The Bathroom
Golf Book

———— • ————

by

Jack Kreismer

RED-LETTER PRESS, INC.
Saddle River, New Jersey

Red-Letter Press, Inc.
P.O. Box 393
Saddle River, NJ 07458

www.Red-LetterPress.com

ACKNOWLEDGMENTS

EDITORIAL:
Jeff Kreismer

•

BOOK DESIGN & TYPOGRAPHY:
Jeff Kreismer

•

COVER ART:
Jeff Godby

•

RESEARCH & DEVELOPMENT:
Kobus Reyneke
Mike Ryan
Jim Tomlinson

The Bathroom Golf Book

The Golfer's Prayer

Now I Lay Me Down To Sleep

I Pray The Lord My Life To Keep

Though I Know You'll Eventually Take My Soul

Please Let Me Prepare At The 19th Hole!

The Front Nine

A Round of Jokes

The guy was a first rate on-the-course and off-the-course louse. When he died, he went to Hell. His eternal punishment was to serve as a caddy for the Devil. This was not your normal golf bag toting duty. The Devil plays with a hot hand... oven-heated golf clubs and balls.

Just as the guy is prepared to caddy for the first time in Hell, he sees a former playing partner, a hideously ugly man, on the first tee with a beautiful woman. The eternally damned caddy mutters out loud, "Why do I have to suffer like this when that guy gets to spend his time with a gorgeous woman like that?" The Devil hears him and says, "Who do you think you are to question that woman's punishment?"

CHIP SHOT

At the first Amateur Championship in 1895, the USGA ruled that Richard Peters would not be able to use his trusty putter- a pool cue.

Bobo the Gorilla was making a fortune for his owner.
They'd travel around to golf courses and challenge
the local pro to a round. The pro would always take
the bet, figuring he could easily beat the
muscle-bound primate. That was, until Bobo
stepped up to the tee and drove the ball 450 yards.
That would usually be enough to scare off the pro,
who'd be willing to settle the bet right then and there
for a discounted sum of money.
One such morning, a top-rated pro conceded the bet
after Bobo hit one of his monstrous drives. "Just out
of curiosity," asked the pro, "how does Bobo putt?"
"The same as he drives... 450 yards."

❖

An alligator was celebrating his 25th year of
guarding a water hazard at a South Florida course.
When the club pro asked him what he would like in
honor of the occasion, the gator replied, "You know,
I've always wanted one of those shirts with a little
picture of Arnold Palmer on the front."

❖

Herb: I got a new set of clubs for my wife.
Harold: Nice trade.

QUICK QUIZ

Who was the first to break 60 in a
professional round of golf?

Al Geiberger, who shot a 59 at the
Danny Thomas-Memphis Classic in 1977

Fred, playing as a single, was teamed with a twosome. Eventually, they asked why he was playing by himself on such a beautiful day.

"My dear wife and I played this course together for over 30 years but this year she passed away. I kept the tee time in her memory."

The twosome were touched at the thoughtfulness of the gesture but one asked him why no one from among her friends and family was willing to take her spot.

"Oh," responded Fred, "they're all at the funeral."

❖

A duffer lived a quarter mile from the local country club. One day he went into the pro shop and bought two dozen balls.

"You want these wrapped?" said the pro shop manager.

"Nah, I'll just drive them home."

❖

A duffer walks into the pro shop and says, "Pete, what can I do to lower my handicap?"

Pete the pro says, "Here, take this."

"But this is just a pencil."

"Yes, but it has an eraser attached."

CHIP SHOT

In 1986, Wayne Grady was disqualified from both the Phoenix Open and the LA Open for hitting someone else's ball.

A small private plane was flying over southwest Florida when all of a sudden the engine died, miles away from any airport.

The pilot turned to his wife and said, "Don't worry honey, there are dozens of golf courses in this area. I'll just land on the next one I see."

To which his wife replied, "What do you mean 'don't worry'? I've seen you play. You'll never hit the fairway!"

❖

Four old golfers took to the links on a Saturday morning as they had every week for the past ten years. The competition was as keen as ever.

On the sixth hole, one of the golfers suddenly collapsed just as he was about to hit a bunker shot. As he lay on the ground, one of the other golfers shouted, "I think Nellie just had a stroke."

Said another player, "Well, just make sure he marks it on his card."

❖

A fellow came home from a round of golf and was greeted at the door by his wife dressed in some very alluring attire.

"Tie me up... and do anything you want," she cooed. So he tied her up and played another round.

QUICK QUIZ

What is an albatross?

It's the British term for a double-eagle.

A golfer goes to a psychiatrist and says, "My wife thinks I'm crazy because I like plaid golf socks." "That's not so strange," says the doc. "I kind of like them, too."

"Really?" exclaimed the patient, excited to find a sympathetic ear. "Do you like yours with chocolate fudge or Hollandaise sauce?"

❖

A terrible golfer hits a ball into a gigantic bunker. He asks his caddy, "What club should I use now?" The caddy says, "The club isn't the important thing. Just make sure to take along plenty of food and water."

❖

The golfer's ball landed in a thicket of weeds in the middle of some woods, an unplayable lie if ever there was one. He tried to line it up but realized it was futile so he picked the ball up and moved it to a better position, shouting to his playing partners, "Found it." Suddenly, he had the feeling he was being watched. He turned around and saw an escaped convict whose picture had been plastered all over the newspaper. The two men looked at each other for a long moment, then the golfer whispered, "Shhhh. I won't tell if you won't."

CHIP SHOT

The Green Zone Golf Club is situated on the border of Finland and Sweden: nine holes are in one country and nine in the other.

A guy was stranded on an island for ages. One day
as he's walking on the beach, a beautiful woman in a
wet suit emerges from the surf.
"Hey, cutie pie. Have you been here long?" she asks.
"I reckon about ten years."
"Do you smoke?"
"Oh, what I'd do for a cigarette!" he responds. With
that, she unzips a pocket in the sleeve of her wet suit,
pulls out a pack of cigarettes, lights one and gives it
to him.
"I guess it's been a long while since you've had a
drink, huh?"
"You got that right," he says.
She pulls out a flask from another pocket, gives it to
him and he takes a swig.
"I bet you haven't played around in a while either,"
she coos as she begins to unzip the front of her wet
suit.
Wide-eyed, he says, "Don't tell me you have a set of
golf clubs in there too!?"

❖

During a particularly crummy round of golf, the
duffer sputtered to his caddy, "I'd move heaven and
earth to break a hundred on this course."
"Try heaven," replied the caddy. "You've already
moved most of the earth."

QUICK QUIZ

"I'd give a bronze to shoot under 70. I
worked too hard for the golds." Who said it:
Michael Phelps, Ryan Lochte or Mark Spitz?

Michael Phelps

A pair of duffers await their turn on the tee, when a drop-dead gorgeous woman in her birthday suit runs across the fairway and into the woods. Two men in white coats and another guy carrying two buckets of sand are chasing after her, and a little old man is bringing up the rear.

"What the heck is going on here?" one of the golfers asks the old geezer.

He says, "She's a nymphomaniac from the funny farm. She keeps trying to escape from the asylum and us attendants are trying to catch her."

The golfer says, "What about that guy with the buckets of sand?"

"Oh, him. That's his handicap. He caught her last time."

❖

At the Sleepy Hollow golf course, a foursome approached the 11th tee where the fairway runs along the edge of the course and adjoins a highway. Forrester teed off and sliced the ball right over the fence. It hit the front tire of a bus and bounced back onto the green and into the cup for a hole-in-one.

"How on earth did you ever get it to bounce off that bus?" asked one of his astonished buddies.

"Well, first off," he replied, "you've got to know the bus schedule."

CHIP SHOT

Approximately 125,000 golf balls are hit into the water at the 17th hole of the Stadium Course at Sawgrass each year.

From the Golf Groaner Hall of Shame:

Q: Why is it so tough to drive a golf ball?
A: It doesn't have a steering wheel.

• • •

A guy in a golf cart yells to the slow-playing foursome ahead, "May I play through? My batteries are low!"

• • •

And then there was the guy whose doctor advised him to play 36 holes a day so he went out and bought a harmonica.

❖

A very prominent CEO of a very big company was sent this ransom message: "If you ever want to see your wife again, bring $100,000 to the 16th green of Deerfield at eleven o'clock sharp tomorrow."
Well, the CEO didn't get there until noon. A masked man jumped out from behind some bushes and snarled, "What took you so long? You're an hour late."
"Hey, cut me some slack," said the CEO. "I have a 25 handicap."

QUICK QUIZ

What famous seaside course was designed by amateur golfer Jack Neville in 1919?

Pebble Beach Golf Links in California

Four old duffers had a Saturday morning eight o'clock tee time for years. On one such morning, they noticed a guy watching them as they teed off. At every tee, he caught up with them and had to wait. When they reached the fifth tee, the guy walked up to the foursome and handed them a card which read, "I am deaf and mute. May I play through?" The old duffers were outraged and signaled to him that nobody plays through their group. He'd just have to bide his time.

On the eighth hole, one of the foursome was in the fairway lining up his second shot. All of the sudden he got bopped in the back of the head by the tremendous force of a golf ball. He turned around and looked back at the tee.

There stood the deaf mute, frantically waving his arm in the air, holding up four fingers.

❖

An executive who often left to play golf during business hours told his secretary to advise all callers that he was away from his desk. A golfer who was part of the executive's foursome forgot where they were playing on one particular day and called the secretary. Loyal to a fault, she'd only say that her boss was away from his desk.

Finally, the exasperated golfer said, "Just tell me. Is he five miles or ten miles away from his desk?"

CHIP SHOT

If you walked all 18 holes of a typical golf course, you'd cover about four miles.

Dear Abby,

I've never written anything like this before, but I desperately need help. I think my wife's been unfaithful to me. She's been going out a lot lately- with "the girls" she says.
The "normal" routine is that one of her "girlfriends" picks her up before I get home from work. Even though I've tried to stay awake to see just who's dropping her off, I always fall asleep on the couch. Last night, though, I decided to do something a little different. I went down to the garage and hid behind my golf clubs so I could get a good view when she arrived home with her "girlfriend."
It was while I was crouched behind my clubs that my dilemma came to light and I need your expert advice. I don't know whether this is a returnable deal or not, or whether I can remedy the problem myself- my driver has a hairline crack right near the club head!

Yours truly,

"Shafted"

❖

Then there was the dyslexic duffer who always wondered how to flog.

QUICK QUIZ

Who won his first major at the 2013 U.S. Open, becoming the first English player to win a major since Nick Faldo in 1996?

Justin Rose

A foreign spaceship hovered over a golf course and two aliens watched a lone duffer in amazement. The golfer hit his tee shot into the rough, took three shots to get back on the fairway, sliced the next one into the woods, and then took two to get back on the fairway again.

Meanwhile, one alien told the other that he must be playing some sort of weird game, and they continued to watch in fascination.

The golfer then hit a shot into a bunker by the green. A few shots later, he made it onto the green. He four-putted to finally get into the hole.

At this juncture, the other alien said to his partner, "Wow! Now he's in serious trouble!"

❖

Three wannabes were taking golf lessons. The first fellow hit the ball far to the right. "That was due to LOFT," remarked the pro.

The second guy hit his ball equally off to the left. "That was due to LOFT," said the pro.

The third golfer teed off and topped the ball. It went just a few yards and stopped. Again, the pro said, "That was due to LOFT."

"LOFT? What exactly do you mean by LOFT?", asked the third guy.

"Lack Of Forseeable Talent," replied the pro.

CHIP SHOT

A portrait of Bobby Jones that hangs at Augusta National Golf Club was painted by Dwight D. Eisenhower.

On a blistering day in South Florida, a priest, a minister and a rabbi were playing golf alongside beautiful Biscayne Bay. As the mercury climbed past 90, 95 and then topped 100 degrees, the men of cloth couldn't take it any longer. The bay looked so inviting that they decided to strip down and jump in the water.

After frolicking and splashing about for a while, they figured that they'd cooled down enough to get back to their game. Before they could dress, a foursome of lady golfers appeared nearby. The minister and priest covered their private parts in a panic but the rabbi just covered his face.

After the women passed by, the priest and minister asked the rabbi why he covered his face instead of his privates.

As the rabbi fastened the last button to his shirt, he replied, "Listen, I don't know about you, but in my congregation it's the face they'll recognize."

❖

A duffer made a terrible shot and, in the process, tore up a gigantic piece of turf. He picked it up, turned to his caddy and said, "What should I do with it?"

The caddy replied, "If I were you, I'd take it home to practice on."

QUICK QUIZ

What's the diameter of a golf ball: 1.68", 1.48", 1.28" or 1.08"?

1.68"

Tiger Woods goes into the 19th hole and spots Stevie Wonder. "Hey, Stevie, it's Tiger. How's your singing career doing these days?"

"I can't complain. How are you hitting 'em?"

Woods responds, "My swing is going real well right now."

Stevie says, "Mine, too."

"What? You play golf?" asks Tiger.

"Sure... I've been playing for years," replies Stevie.

"But you're blind," Woods says. "How can you possibly play?"

Wonder replies, "I get my caddy to stand in the middle of the fairway and holler to me. When I hear the sound of his voice, I play the ball toward him. Then, after I get to where the ball lands, the caddy moves down to the green and again I play the ball toward his voice."

"But how do you putt?" asks Tiger.

"Simple... My caddy lies down in front of the hole and calls to me with his head on the ground. And then I play the ball toward his voice," explains Stevie.

"What's your handicap, Stevie?"

Stevie responds, "I'm a scratch golfer."

Woods says, "We've got to play a round sometime."

"Sure, but people don't take me seriously, so I only play for money - never for less than $5,000 a hole."

"You're on. When would you like to play?" asks Woods.

Stevie says, "Pick a night."

CHIP SHOT

In 2006, South Carolina's 12-year-old Blake Hadden recorded two holes-in-one at the Future Masters. Hadden aced the 83-yard 5th hole and the 140-yard 11th hole at the Dothan Country Club in Alabama.

Golf is what you play when you're too out of shape to play softball.

❖

At a hoity toity country club which strictly enforces its rules, a member saw a guest of the club place his ball five inches in front of the tee markers.
The member hurriedly went over to the guest and said, "Sir, I don't know whether you've ever played here before, but we have very stringent rules about placing your tee at or behind the markers before driving the ball."
The guest looked the snooty club member right in the eye and retorted, "First, I've never played here before. Second, I don't care about your rules. And third, this is my second shot."

❖

A golf club walks into a bar and asks for a beer.
The bartender refuses to serve him.
"Why not?" demands the golf club.
"Because you'll be driving later."

❖

Duffer: That can't be my ball. It's too old.

Caddy: It's been a long time since we teed off, sir.

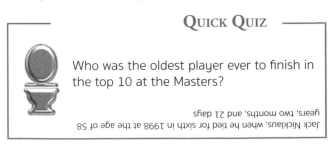

QUICK QUIZ

Who was the oldest player ever to finish in the top 10 at the Masters?

Jack Nicklaus, when he tied for sixth in 1998 at the age of 58 years, two months, and 21 days

A man went to a therapist for a consultation about an obsession that was ruining his health. "It's golf, Doc. Golf is destroying me. I'm desperate. I can't even escape it in my sleep. As soon as I close my eyes, I'm out there sinking a two-foot putt or making a magnificent drive right down the fairway. When I wake up in the morning, I'm even more tired than I was before I went to bed. What am I going to do? Can you help me?"

The therapist answered reassuringly, "First of all, you are going to have to make a conscious effort not to dream about golf. For example, when you close your eyes at night, try to imagine something else exciting, like discovering a gold mine or sailing on an around-the-world cruise."

The patient replied, "That's easy for you to say, Doc. If I do that, I'll miss my tee-time."

❖

Two old golfers were reminiscing as they played. One pointed towards the woods. "My first girlfriend was named Mary Katherine Agnes Colleen Patricia Marion Margaret Kathleen O'Shaugnessey. Back when I was a lad, working as a caddie, I carved her name in one of those trees right over there."

"What ever happened?" asked his friend.

"The tree fell on me."

CHIP SHOT

In 1973, Arthur Thompson shot a round of 103 at the Uplands Golf Course in British Columbia. Not bad for a man who was 103 years old.

Two golfers are standing on the 10th tee. Jerry takes about 20 practice swings, changes his grip five or six times, and adjusts his stance just as much.

"Hey, Jerry! Play, for heaven's sake. We don't have all day," says Larry.

"Hold on a minute, I gotta do this right. See the woman standing up there on the clubhouse porch? That's my mother-in-law and I would like to get off the perfect shot," says Jerry.

Larry looks, and about 250 yards away he sees the woman. "You must be kidding. You couldn't possibly hit her from here."

❖

Two duffers are downing a few at the 19th hole when one says to the other, "I'm taking my wife to the Holy Land to walk where the saints once walked." The second duffer says, "Oh, you're taking her to Jerusalem?"

"Jerusalem? Heck no. I'm taking her to St Andrews."

❖

Did you hear about the politically correct country club? They don't refer to their golfers as having handicaps. Instead, they're "stroke challenged."

QUICK QUIZ

What golfer was married briefly to former tennis star Chris Evert?

Greg Norman

Q and As

Q: How many golfers does it take to change a light bulb?

A: FORE!

Q: What did the Ancient Romans yell on the golf course?

A: "IV!"

Q: When is the course too wet to play?

A: When your golf cart capsizes

Q: How many golfers does it take to screw in a light bulb?

A: Two- One to do it and the other to tell him that he looked up.

Q: What is the easiest shot in golf?

A: Your fourth putt

Q: What type of engine do they use in golf carts?

A: Fore cylinder

Q: What do hackers and condemned playgrounds have in common?

A: Lousy swings

CHIP SHOT

The 365 acres that house the Augusta National Golf Club were purchased by Bobby Jones and fellow investors for $70,000 in 1931.

Ned and Mack were very competitive at golf and very closely matched. One day they decided on a "play it as it lies" round to break the deadlock.
The number one hole was a par 4 and both players drove it right down the middle, about 250 yards.
They drove the golf cart up for the second shot and Ned hit a great shot to the green within 12 feet of the hole.
Mack, however, sliced his over the trees and right onto the cart path of the adjoining hole.
"Well, I guess I get a free drop from the cart path," Mack said.
Ned pointed out that it was a strict "Play it as it lays" game and so he drove up to the green to finish and Mack drove to his ball over on the cart path.
Ned putted his ball in easily and looked up to see Mack taking wild practice swings which sent up showers of sparks. He chuckled at his opponent's misfortune until Mack took a perfect swing and sent the ball flying right into the cup.
With that, Mack drove back to the green to pick up Ned. "That was amazing!" Ned exclaimed. "A fantastic shot- and after all those sparks. What club did you use?"
Mack just smiled and said, "Your five iron."

QUICK QUIZ

Regulations call for a golf hole to be how wide in diameter: 3.25", 4.25" or 5.25"?

4.25"

Higgins was frantic and called his doctor. "Doc, it's Higgins. I've got an emergency. My baby just swallowed my golf tees!"
"I'll be right there!" exclaimed the doctor.
"But what do I do in the meantime?" cried Higgins.
"Practice your putting."

❖

Here's one from the star of *Caddyshack*- the man who got no respect- Rodney Dangerfield:
"Every time my wife takes the car there's trouble. The other day she came home, there were 100 dents in the car. She said she took a shortcut through the driving range."

❖

Rodney was playing golf with a priest when a sudden storm blew up. The desperate pair found shelter in an old toolshed with a leaky roof, and as the lightning struck all around them, they saw a roaring tornado bearing down on the shed.
"Father," pleaded Rodney, "I don't want to die! Can't you do something about this?"
"Sorry," said the priest. "I'm in sales, not management."

CHIP SHOT

A golf cart is started and stopped an average of 150 times during a round of golf.

A coroner examined the corpse of the golfer's wife, then began interrogating the husband. "Is that your Top-Flite that's embedded in the temple of the deceased?"

"Yes, it is," the golfer admitted.

"And why is there a second Top-Flite embedded in her back?"

The golfer answered, "The temple shot was my mulligan."

❖

Two psychologically fragile fellows are avid duffers who, coincidentally, have the same shrink who's prescribed the same treatment for them- a game of golf using an imaginary ball to reduce stress.

The two are paired together and tee off with their imaginary balls. Both hit magnificent imaginary drives down the middle of the fairway and wind up birdying the first hole. This continues throughout the round, a birdie here, an eagle there for each of them. Finally, they reach the 18th hole dead even. Both of them hit tee shots that have their imaginary balls land on the green. The first guy lines up his "46-foot" putt and sinks the imaginary ball. He says to his playing partner, "Let's see what you can do now. The best you can hope for is a tie."

"I don't think so," his partner says matter of factly. "You just used my ball."

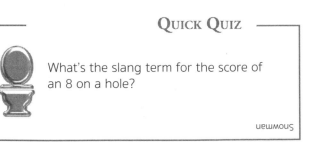

QUICK QUIZ

What's the slang term for the score of an 8 on a hole?

Snowman

Wife: I have some bad news and some worse news.

Hubby: What's the bad news?

Wife: I ran over your clubs.

Hubby: Geez! What's the worse news?

Wife: They were on the front porch.

❖

A guy goes to the doctor for a checkup. Afterwards, the doctors says, "I've got good news and bad news."

The guy says, "Give me the bad news first, Doc."

"You've got an incurable disease and probably won't live more than a year."

"Geez, what could possibly be the good news?"

"I broke 80 yesterday."

❖

Barrington: I say, did you hear what happened to Rockingham?

Hyde-White: No, I'm afraid I haven't.

Barrington: He was awakened in the middle of the night by a burglar and beat the miscreant into submission with a five-iron.

Hyde-White: Do tell. How many strokes?

CHIP SHOT

In 1954, Laddie Lukas shot an 87 at the Sandy Lodge Golf Course in England - a decent performance, but it was really extraordinary considering what he was wearing - a blindfold.

While attending a conference in deepest, darkest Africa, a businessman found himself with some spare time. Since he had played golf on three other continents, he wanted to add Africa to his lifetime list. Finding the local golf course at the edge of the jungle, he asked the pro if he could get on.

"Of course," said the pro. "What's your handicap?" The businessman was always a bit sensitive in that area and decided to drop it from 18 to 16 but was puzzled as to why they even asked.

"It's very important that we know," said the pro, who then called a caddy. "This gentleman's handicap is a 16," he told the caddy. He then bid the businessman good luck and went on his way.

The businessman was surprised at the constant references to his handicap as well as the fact that the caddy carried a large rifle, but he decided not to ask any questions.

On the first hole the caddy advised him that it was important to avoid the trees to the right. Naturally, the businessman hit directly into the trees and while he was looking for his ball, he heard a shot whizz by over his head and a huge snake fell dead at his feet. "Black Mamba," the caddy said. "Deadliest snake in Africa."

On the next hole, the caddy cautioned him to stay clear of the brush on the left and of course, the businessman hit right into it. While retrieving the ball, he felt the hot breath of a roaring lion on his neck

QUICK QUIZ

According to *Golf Digest*, the odds of doing this twice in a single round of golf are 67 million-to-one.

Making a hole-in-one

just before a shot rang out, nicking the lion's ear and scaring it off.

"Saved your life again," the caddy said. "Now whatever you do on this next hole, stay away from the lake."

Sure enough, on the next hole, the businessman missed the green and the ball rolled down to the edge of the lake. As the businessman was preparing to swing, a huge crocodile lunged from the water and snapped off his leg below the knee.

As he lay there in horrific pain, trying to fashion a tourniquet from his belt, the businessman cried out, "Why didn't you shoot him?!"

The caddy replied quite matter-of-factly, "Sorry sir, this is the 17th handicap hole. You don't get a shot here."

And that golfers, is why you should never, ever lie about your handicap.

❖

"You're going out to play golf again?" sighed the golf widow.

"But Honey, I'm under doctor's orders," the husband replied as he stopped in the doorway.

"How dumb do you think I am?" the wife asked.

"Really dear, it's true. At my last checkup he told me to get plenty of iron every day."

Chip Shot

After winning the 1949 L.A. Open, Lloyd Mangrum dropped his pants before the media to reveal why he won- lucky pajama bottoms!

Negotiations were at a standstill between Big Joey Gabone, representing the union, and Morris Brathwaite, representing management. Braithwaite was accusing union members of abusing their contract's sick leave provisions. Gabone categorically denied it.

The next morning, Brathwaite showed up at the talks waving the local newspaper. "Here, look at the sports page," said Brathwaite. "This photo of a golfer under the headline 'Local Man Breaks Club Record' -That man is a union member and he called in sick yesterday."

The room fell silent for a few moments and Brathwaite felt quite self-satisfied until Gabone piped up with, "Unbelievable!"

"Oh you can believe it," crowed Brathwaite, "Pictures don't lie."

"I know," said Gabone. "Imagine how well this guy would have played if he hadn't been sick!"

❖

A golfer sliced his ball right off the course, hitting a lawyer who was walking down a nearby sidewalk. The golfer ran over to the stricken lawyer to see if he was okay. "Im going to sue you for $5,000," the lawyer said.

"I'm awfully sorry, but I yelled 'Fore!'"

"I'll take it!" the lawyer replied.

QUICK QUIZ

Trailing by seven strokes on the final day, who shot a record-tying 64 to win his third green jacket at Augusta in 1978?

Gary Player

A priest, a doctor and a lawyer were becoming frustrated with the slow play of the foursome ahead of them. "What's with these guys?" the lawyer grumbled. "We've been waiting to tee off at least 15 minutes."

"Here comes the greenskeeper," said the priest. "Let's have a word with him."

When confronted, the greenskeeper advised them that the slow-playing group were firefighters and that, sadly, they all lost their sight while saving the clubhouse from a fire a year ago. In gratitude, the club allowed them to play for free anytime.

The priest expressed his concern and said he'd keep them in his prayers. The doctor volunteered to contact an ophthalmologist buddy to see if there was anything he could do for them.

The lawyer said, "Why can't these guys play at night?"

❖

An expectant mother who was a couple of weeks overdue was told by her doctor to walk as much as possible every morning until the baby came. The M.D. also advised her husband that he should go along just in case anything started.

"Alright, Doc," replied the husband. "But would it be okay if she carries my clubs while she walks?"

CHIP SHOT

Mr. Steven Ward shot a 222 at the 6,212-yard Pecos Course in Reeves County, Texas, on June 18, 1976.
At the time, Mr. Ward was 3 years old.

Albert had a bad day of golf- a really bad day. As he was walking through the parking lot on his way out, he was stopped by a policeman. "Excuse me sir, did you tee off on the 17th hole about a half hour ago?" "Why yes, yes I did," Albert answered.

"And you hooked your ball over the trees and off the course?"

"I did," Albert answered.

The policeman continued, "Then it was your ball which went through the windshield of a station wagon, causing it to stop suddenly and cause a chain reaction collision involving eight cars. This resulted in a truck jack-knifing and blocking the road so that a fire engine couldn't get through, causing an apartment building to burn to the ground. So... What do you intend to do about it?"

Albert shook his head sadly and said, "The only thing I can do Officer. I've got to close my stance a bit, tighten my grip and lower my right thumb."

❖

"Father," the young man said to the priest, "is it a sin to play golf on Sunday?"

"My son," replied the padre, placing his hand on the fellow's shoulder, "the way you play golf, it's a sin any day."

QUICK QUIZ

Which of the four majors was known as "Glory's last shot" until 2019?

The PGA Championship, which was moved up on the calendar

The only blonde golf joke in the book:

A blonde goes into the pro shop and asks the
manager, "Do you have any green golf balls?"
"No, we don't carry any green golf balls."
The blonde says, "Why not?"
The manager responds, "The question should be
more like 'Why would we?'"
"Isn't it obvious?" the blonde says with a smirk.
"They're easier to find in the sand trap."

❖

At his 50th wedding anniversary party held at the
local country club, Ralph was asked the secret of his
long marriage. He stood up before his assembled
crowd of friends and relatives and shared his marital
philosophy.
"Gertrude and I have made it a practice throughout
our long marriage to play golf and then go out for
two romantic, candlelit dinners a week - right here at
this country club. Unfailingly, twice a week, we come
here and enjoy the delicious food and soft music.
We soak up the ambiance of this fine establishment
and sip a vintage wine. She goes Thursdays and I go
Fridays."

❖

CHIP SHOT

The U.S. Open was first televised in 1947,
the British Open in 1955, and The Masters in
1956.

Morty and Fred were teeing off early one summer's day when the usual tranquility of the golf course was shattered by the siren of an ambulance racing to the maternity hospital atop a nearby hill.

"Somebody's getting a big surprise today," said Morty.

"I'll say," replied Fred as he lined up his putt. "When I left this morning, my wife's contractions were still at least an hour apart."

❖

A politician died and, as might be expected, he went straight to Hell. As Satan was showing him around the place, he noticed a beautiful golf course that would put Augusta to shame. Being a lifelong golf fanatic, he was thrilled. Striding into the pro shop, he spotted a sign that read, "Only the Finest Equipment and All Absolutely FREE – Help Yourself."

Having selected a fantastic set of matched clubs and a first class golf bag, he next needed a caddy. The caddy shack was filled with gorgeous women who were movie stars in life. He chose Marilyn Monroe, who was wearing a teddy. He couldn't wait to begin his dream game! As he stepped up to the tee, he reached into the ball pocket and found it empty. He looked up to see Satan grinning from ear to ear.

"Don't bother going back to the pro shop. There are no balls anywhere – you see, that's the hell of it."

QUICK QUIZ

Two men have tied for the lowest 72-hole score in a major, 264. One did it at the PGA Championship in 2018, the other in the 2016 British Open. Can you name either golfer?

Brooks Koepka, in 2018 and Henrik Stenson, in 2016

Bumper Snickers

• GOLFERS EXPRESS THEMSELVES TO A TEE

• GOLF COURSES ARE OFTEN GROUNDS FOR DIVORCE

• I BRAKE FOR ANIMALS BUT SINK BIRDIES

• MY OTHER CAR IS A GOLF CART

• GOLF SEPARATES THE MEN FROM THE POISE

• CAUTION: GOLFER AT WHEEL- DRIVER IN TRUNK

• MAY THE COURSE BE WITH YOU

• IF YOU THINK I'M A LOUSY DRIVER, YOU SHOULD SEE ME PUTT

• I'D RATHER BE DRIVING MY GOLF BALL

❖

Maybe you've heard about the duffer who's so bad, he has an unplayable lie when he tees up.

CHIP SHOT

Sergio Garcia, who sank his first hole in one in 2012, has been coming up aces for a long time. Garcia's an avid poker player and has played on the Poker Stars tour.

One-Liners on the Links

• Golf is the most popular way of beating around the bush.

• A caddie is a lie-detector.

• Golf is nature's way of telling you, "This is what life looks like from behind a tree."

• You can judge a man by the golf score he keeps.

• Golf is a very popular game- the only sport that can convert a duck pond into a water hazard.

• The one advantage bowling has over golf is that you very rarely lose the ball.

• Whoever said golf was fun either has never played golf or has never had any fun.

❖

"You better have a good excuse for coming home at this time of the night," demanded the duffer's wife. "I was playing golf with Larry and Bart," answered the hubbie.
"What!? At two o'clock in the morning?"
"Yes," he said. "Nightclubbing."

QUICK QUIZ

In 2013, who became the first Australian to win The Masters when he defeated Angel Cabrera in a two-hole playoff?

Adam Scott

A guy applies for a sales position with a big golf equipment manufacturer. While he's waiting for the interview, the receptionist tells him, "You seem like a nice guy. Let me give you a tip. My boss is very sensitive about the fact that he doesn't have any ears. At some point, he's going to ask you if you notice anything odd about him. Whatever you do, don't make any mention of the ears."

The guy thanks the receptionist for the advice and goes in for the interview. Well, the boss is very impressed with the guy's resume, his knowledge of the game in general and of golf gear in particular. But sure enough, at one point the boss says, "Tell me. Do you notice anything different about me?"

The guy looks at the boss and responds, "Well, now that you mention it, I can tell you're wearing contact lenses."

"That's amazing. I like perceptiveness in my employees. But how on earth did you know I wear contacts?"

"Easy. You'd be wearing glasses if you had any ears."

❖

Of course, you've heard about the foursome that was so bad they called themselves "The Bronchitis Brothers" because they were just a bunch of hackers.

─────── CHIP SHOT ───────

Seve Ballesteros was disqualified from the 1980 U.S. Open after a traffic tie-up caused him to arrive late at the first tee.

McMurphy's Laws

We all know Murphy's Law, but only golfers can truly appreciate "McMurphy's Laws of the Links."

1. No matter how bad your last shot was, the worst is yet to come. This law extends far beyond the 18th hold to the course of a tournament, and ultimately, an entire lifetime.

2. Your best round of golf will be immediately followed by your worst round ever. The probability of the latter increases in direct proportion with the number of people you tell about the former.

3. Brand new golf balls are irresistibly attracted to water. The more expensive the ball, the greater the attraction.

4. "Nice lag" can be translated to "lousy putt." By the same token, "tough break" translates to "I can't believe you missed that last one, bonehead."

5. Palm trees eat golf balls.

6. Sand is alive. It's an evil, malevolent presence which exists solely to make golfers' lives miserable. Sand is Demon Dust.

QUICK QUIZ

The winner of what tournament receives the Francis D. Ouimet Memorial Trophy?

The U.S. Senior Open

7. Golf balls never bounce off trees back into play. If one ever does happen to, you can bet the devil will be teeing off in six inches of snow.

8. There is a point on every golf course that is the absolute furthest from the clubhouse. You'll know you are there when your cart runs out of juice.

9. The person you would most hate to lose to will always be the one who beats you.

10. Golf should be sworn off at least three times a month...and sworn at the rest of the time.

❖

A guy walks into the 19th hole and orders two martinis. The bartender serves them and says, "If it's all the same to you, buddy, I could have made a double and used one glass."
The guy says, "Oh, I know, but my golfing partner died and, just before he did, I promised him I'd order him a drink after each round of golf."
The next week the guy comes back and says to the bartender, "I'll have a martini."
The bartender says, "And one for your buddy, too?"
He says, "Oh, no. This is for my buddy. I'm on the wagon."

Chip Shot

Survey Says: 7 out of 10 golfers claim they've either had their clubs stolen or know of someone who has.

The Top Ten Ways To Tell You're A Golf Widow

10. When hubby refers to his "better half", he's talking about the back nine.

9. If you ever had to skip town after a golf bet went sour

8. He forgets your anniversary but annually marks the observance of the day he first played at Pebble Beach.

7. If you've ever had to put the 19th hole on speed-dial

6. The only dimples he appreciates anymore are on golf balls.

5. He tells you that you deserve a second honeymoon and then leaves you on a golf vacation.

4. If going out as a foursome never includes you

3. His idea of renewing his vows is telling you exactly what he yelled after missing that two-foot putt.

QUICK QUIZ

Name the woman who became the youngest ever to win an LPGA major tournament when she won the 2015 Evian Championship.

Lydia Ko

2. You don't need the Weather Channel. If he's home, it's raining.

And the NUMBER ONE way to tell if you're a golf widow...
When he says he's going out to "play a round," you almost wish he would.

• • •

What are the four worst words you could hear during a game of golf?

"It's still your turn."

❖

Did you hear about the divorce lawyer who did a mailing to all the married male members of the exclusive country club?
She sent out 175 Valentines signed "Guess who?"

❖

And then there was the guy who had the great short game. Unfortunately, it was off the tee.

CHIP SHOT

Built in 1895, the Van Cortlandt Park Golf Course in the Bronx (N.Y.) was the first public golf course in the U.S.

One day, the devil approached a golfer and said, "How'd you like to make a hole-in-one to impress your buddies?"

"What's the catch?" asked the fellow suspiciously.

"It'll shorten your love life by five years," grinned the devil.

"Hmmm. All right, I'll do it," agreed the man. He then went on to make one of the most spectacular shots ever and aced the hole. A few minutes later, the devil approached the man on the following tee.

"How'd you like to go for two in a row?"

"At what cost?" asked the man.

"This'll shorten your love life by ten years."

"You drive a tough bargain, but okay," replied the golfer, who strode to the tee and sent a 310-yard beauty right into the cup.

At the next tee, the devil appeared once again. "This is a once in a lifetime offer. If you ace this one, it'll be three straight holes-in-one. It's never been done before in the history of the world. But it's gonna cost you another 20 years off your love life."

"Let's go for it," said the man, who proceeded to dazzle everyone by hitting the ball from behind his back, sending it over a huge pond onto the green and right into the hole.

It was such an amazing shot that even the devil himself applauded.

And that's how Father O'Malley got into the *Guinness Book of World Records.*

QUICK QUIZ

Can you name the golf course which is named after a Dutch farmer who once owned the land? (Hint: Jack Nicklaus won two of his four U.S. Opens there, in 1967 and 1980.)

Baltusrol, in Springfield, New Jersey (The farmer's name was Baltus Roll.)

Then there was the bachelor who preferred golf to women. Even so, he finally found the love of his life and got married. You might say he learned to put his heart before the course.

❖

Golfer: I think I'm going to drown myself in the lake.
Caddy: Think you can keep your head down that long?

❖

The newcomer to the course was studying the ball and its distance from the green. "What do you think?" he asked the caddy.
"Well, yesterday I caddied for Jerry Seinfeld. He hits 'em about like you. I advised him to use an eight-iron."
With that, the golfer took out his eight-iron, addressed the ball and played his shot- a shot that fell far short of the green.
The angry golfer said, "I thought you told Jerry Seinfeld to use an eight."
"I did. He didn't reach the green either."

❖

CHIP SHOT

Sam Snead's PGA Tour victories span a record 29 years, from his first win in 1936 to his last in 1965.

Taking some well-deserved time off from their
heavenly duties, Moses and St. Peter hit the links to
indulge themselves in a game of golf. Moses teed up
and hit a beautiful shot right down the fairway to the
green, about two feet from the hole. St. Peter,
however, whacked a bad hook, which disappeared
into the woods.

Moses was smiling smugly when an eagle emerged
from high over a nearby Interstate and dropped
St. Peter's ball into the exhaust stack of a passing
tractor-trailer. The pressure buildup soon shot the
ball back into the air, where it was struck by
lightning from some low-lying clouds. That sent the
ball careening off a few chimneys, and it ricocheted
right back to the golf course, landed on the green
and rolled right into the hole.

Moses sighed, turned to a smiling St. Peter and said,
"Oh, c'mon- not when we're playing for money!"

❖

A lawyer mailed a note to his client:

Dear Mr. Foxworth:
Thought I saw you at the 19th hole yesterday... Went
over to your table to say hello, but it wasn't you so I
went back. One twentieth of an hour: $20.

QUICK QUIZ

What golfer's first major win came at the
age of 42 at the 1992 U.S. Open?

Tom Kite

"Why do you keep looking at your watch?" the annoyed duffer asked his caddy.
"It's not a watch, sir. It's a compass."

❖

Manny, playing in a two-ball foursome, drove his tee shot to the edge of the green on a par three hole. Ralph, playing the second shot, managed to chip it over the green into a bunker.
Undaunted, Manny recovered with a fine shot to within three feet of the hole. Ralph missed the easy putt, leaving Manny to finish the hole.
"Do you realize we took five strokes on an easy par three?" said Manny.
"Yes, and don't forget who took three of them!" replied Ralph.

❖

A duffer sliced a ball into a field of chickens and struck one of the hens, killing it instantly. He was terribly bothered by it and reported the disaster to the farmer.
"I'm so sorry," he said. "My horrible tee shot hit one of your hens and killed it. Please allow me to replace the chicken, okay?"
"I'm not sure," replied the farmer, as he thought it over. "How many eggs a day do you lay?"

CHIP SHOT

Arguably the most famous left-handed golfer of all-time, Phil Mickelson is naturally right-handed.

Golfer's Horoscope

Aquarius (Jan 20-Feb 18) The Golf Club
Born under the sign of the country club, you are
industrious, prosperous and like to wear funny pants-
and you love to pull the old "dead mouse in the
golfbag" trick on the newest member of the club.

Pisces (Feb 19-Mar 20) The Sand Trap
You are a child of the sand trap. You are drawn to
the rough and to water hazards. This is because in a
former life, you were either Lewis or Clark.

Aries (Mar 21-Apr 19) The Golf Tee
Born under the sign of the tee, you came into the
world along with the spring- which explains why the
smell of newly mowed grass follows you everywhere.
It's all those divots!

Taurus (Apr 20-May 20) The Golf Ball
Born under the sign of the golf ball, you tend to be
round and dimpled all over.

Gemini (May 21-Jun 21) The Golf Swing
Like all Gemini golfers, you have a tendency to stand
too close to the ball. Unfortunately, that's also true
after you've hit it.

Cancer (Jun 22-Jul 22) The 19th Hole
The summer heat means that you are one of the
chosen children of the 19th Hole. Trading golf balls
for highballs, you play a round, then buy one.

QUICK QUIZ

Tiger Woods won the 2019 Masters at the
age of 43, becoming its second-oldest
winner. Jack Nicklaus was the oldest to win
the green jacket at what age in 1986?

46

Leo (Jul 23-Aug 22) The Driving Range
Your life is intimately tied up with the game. Sadly, the best drive you'll ever make is in a golf cart.

Virgo (Aug 23-Sep 22) The Scorecard
A Scorecardian, you are good with numbers... a talent you put to good use in cheating.

Libra (Sep 23-Oct 23) The Water Hazard
You are forever losing your ball in the drink. You have such an amazing ability at finding the water that your golfing companions refer to your woods as "diving sticks."

Scorpio (Oct 24-Nov 21) The Golf Shoe
You are tremendously gifted at golf. In fact, you immediately master any hole you attempt... especially the ones with windmills.

Sagittarius (Nov 22-Dec 21) The Glove
Though your tee time is late in the year, you are devoted to your sport. This is a shame because, basically, you stink!

Capricorn (Dec 22-Jan 19) The Fairway
Though you have much power, you are horribly inconsistent. In fact, you would do well to hit your first drive before deciding which course you'll be playing that day.

CHIP SHOT

Only 20% of golfers have a handicap below 18.

Old Cornwaithe was playing alone at Pebble Beach one foggy day when he heard a voice from the nearby water hazard.

"Hey, Mister," the voice said.

He looked around but saw no one, so he resumed his slow creak towards the green.

A few seconds later, he heard, "Hey, Mister," again. He parted the tall grass at the edge of the water and looked down at a frog perched on a leaf.

The frog said, "Yeah, it's me."

"So what do you want, frog?" the old man sneered.

"Listen, Mister," the frog replied. "I'm really a beautiful princess, but an evil witch has cast a spell upon me and turned me into an ugly, slimy frog. All I need is a kiss and I'll turn back into a gorgeous princess. Pick me up, kiss me and then I'm all yours."

With that, the old man scooped up the frog and slipped her in his golf bag.

"Hey, Mister," the frog protested. "Aren't you going to kiss me? What about all the fun you can have with me?"

"Thanks just the same," Cornwaithe responded, "but at my age, I'd just as soon have a talking frog."

❖

And then there was the Microsoft head honcho who excelled at golf, particularly with his hard drive.

QUICK QUIZ

What state has the most golf courses in the U.S.?

Florida

Charlie showed up for an early tee time looking exhausted.

"Hey Charlie, what happened?" asked his golfing buddy.

"Oh, I had a big fight with my wife," he replied, still a bit dazed.

"I thought your wife was out of town last night."

"Yeah," Charlie answered ruefully. "So did I."

❖

Old Findley finally went to that big golf course in the sky, leaving an estate of $200,000. After all his final expenses were paid at the funeral home, his widow confided to her closest friend that there was nothing left.

"Nothing?!" the woman asked incredulously. "How can that be? You said he had $200,000."

"Well," replied the widow Findley, "the funeral cost $8,000 and there was the matter of $2,000 back dues at the country club. The rest went for the memorial stone."

"$190,000 for a memorial stone?! That's unbelievable. How big was it?"

The widow smiled and sighed, "Oh, just over seven carats."

CHIP SHOT

In 2013, 77-year-old Gary Player became the oldest athlete ever to appear naked in the "Body Issue" of *ESPN The Magazine*.

A golfer, playing one of the wilder courses in Alaska, was suddenly confronted by an angry grizzly bear. "Oh, God! I'm doomed," he cried out. Just then, a voice boomed out from above.

"This is God. You are not doomed, my son. You must smite the great bear on the nose with your fists."

Unflinchingly, the golfer obeyed and landed a few good roundhouse punches on the bear's snout.

"Now you must gouge out its eyes," God commanded.

The golfer reached up and forced his thumbs into the bear's eyes as hard as he could.

"Now strike a great blow to the beast's head with your golf club," God instructed.

The golfer cracked the snarling bruin right between the eyes, causing the bear to rear up on its hind legs in a fury and bare its huge teeth.

"What now, God?" pleaded the golfer.

"Now, my son," God replied, "now you are doomed."

❖

Q: What's the difference between a golfer and a fisherman?

A: When a golfer lies, he doesn't have to bring anything home to prove it.

QUICK QUIZ

Of the 13 original inductees into the World Golf Hall of Fame in 1974, two were women. Can you name either of them?

Patty Berg and Babe Didrikson Zaharias

A minister and his very conservative wife had a great marriage, except for his long business trips and lifelong obsession with golf.

One day while he was away, she was cleaning and found a box of mementos in the back of the bedroom closet. In it she found three golf balls and $800.

That night when he called, she asked him the meaning of the three golf balls. He said, "Well dear, I've been keeping that box for 20 years. I'm ashamed to admit it, but so great is my passion for the game of golf that occasionally I swear on the course. Every time I use unsavory language, I penalize myself one golf ball."

Shocked that her husband, a man of the cloth, would ever use four-letter words, the wife was at first taken aback but then thought, "Well, three balls means that he's only cursed three times in 20 years. I suppose that isn't so bad."

"All right dear," she said, "I forgive you for your lapses, but tell me, what's the $800 for?"

"Oh that," answered the minister. "I found a guy who buys golf balls at two bucks a dozen."

❖

Then there was the hunter who got a hole-in-one but went crazy trying to figure out how to mount it.

CHIP SHOT

South Korea's Gunsan Country Club boasts the longest golf hole in the world. Its 3rd hole is a par 7, 1,097 yards!

"Golf, golf, golf. That's all you ever think about," griped the newlywed bride at the dinner table. "You've been on the golf course every single day of our honeymoon."
"Sweetheart," cooed her husband in his most soothing tone as he reached across the table to take her hand. "Believe me, golf is the last thing on my mind at this moment. Now please stop this silliness and let's get back to our meal. Would you please pass the putter?"

❖

Gale: I played golf with my boss the other day.

Howard: How'd it go?

Gale: Well, on the first hole, the boss topped the ball and only sent it about 20 feet, leaving it 375 yards from the hole.

Howard: What'd you do?

Gale: I conceded the putt.

❖

They're at the 19th hole, watching the live telecast of the British Open when someone says, "Turn up the sound."
Someone else replies, "Ssssh...not while McIlroy is putting."

QUICK QUIZ

How old must you be to play on the Champions Tour?

05

Phone conversation at the 19th hole:

"Hello, Fairleigh Golf Club. I'd like to find out if my husband is there."

"No ma'am."

"You haven't even heard my name. How can you possibly know he isn't there?"

"Because ma'am, no husband is ever here when his wife calls."

❖

Two duffers were on the third tee. One hit his ball in the rough and went to find it while the other hopped in the cart to head down the fairway. Minutes later, there was no sign of the golfer in the rough, so his buddy hopped back in the cart and then found his friend buried up to his waist in quicksand.

"Stay still. I'll go get a rope to pull you out," said the second golfer.

"No, no! Quick- bring me a sand wedge!"

❖

Caddy: I'm terribly sorry, sir. I think we're lost.

Matty: Lost?! You told me you're the best caddy on the course.

Caddy: But we've been off the course for half an hour!

Chip Shot

Jack Nicklaus made his debut on the PGA Tour at the 1962 Los Angeles Open. He finished last in the money, earning $33.33.

Duffer: What do you think I should give my caddy for his birthday?

Partner: Your clubs.

❖

Wally: I'll never play golf with my banker again.

Oscar: Why not?

Wally: Every time I yell "Fore," he yells "Closure."

❖

A group of golfers were putting when all of the sudden a ball dropped on the green. One of the duffers winked at the others and kicked the ball into the hole.

Moments later, a very overweight, out of shape and out of breath fellow appeared on the green. He looked around distractedly and asked, "Anyone seen my ball?"

"Yeah, it went in the hole," said the poker-faced jokester.

The heavyset fellow looked at him with disbelief. He waddled over to the hole, looked in, reached down and picked up his ball. Then he looked down the fairway and excitedly yelled to his playing partner, "Hey, Bernie, I got a 12!"

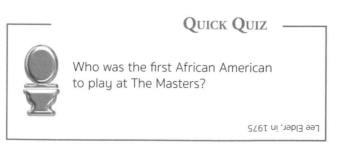

QUICK QUIZ

Who was the first African American to play at The Masters?

Lee Elder, in 1975

A guy went to a psychiatrist and announced, "There's nothing wrong with me, Doc, but my wife says if I don't come see you, she's getting a divorce."

"And exactly what does she think is the matter?" asked the shrink.

"Well," the new patient replied, "you see, I'm Jack Nicklaus and she seems to think there's something wrong with that."

A bit surprised, the psychiatrist asked, "Jack Nicklaus, as in the world-famous golfer?"

"Yep, that's me."

Knowing full well that the patient sitting before him was not Jack Nicklaus, the doctor prescribed three therapy sessions a week. After two years of this intensive treatment, the psychiatrist announced to his patient, "Congratulations, you're cured."

"Congratulations for what?" grumbled his patient. "Before I came to you, I was Jack Nicklaus. Now I'm a nobody."

❖

A man tees up at the first hole. All of a sudden, a woman wearing a bridal gown comes running toward him. "You bum! You bum!" she screams. "Aw, c'mon, dear," he says. "I told you only if it rains."

CHIP SHOT

In 1962, Australian meteorologist Nils Leid hit a golf ball 2,640 yards across the ice in Antarctica. That's approximately a one and a half mile tee shot!

A priest was in the middle of the fairway when he heard a golfer yell "Fore!" just a moment before a ball smacked into his back. The duffer who made the drive came rushing toward the priest to apologize. When the priest assured the fellow that he was fine, the golfer smiled and exclaimed, "Thank God, Father! I've been at this game for 30 years and I can finally tell my pals that I've hit my first holy one!"

❖

Standing on the tee of a long par three, the confident golfer said to his caddy, "Looks like a four-wood and a putt to me."
The caddy handed him the four-wood, with which the golfer topped the ball about 15 yards in front of the tee. Immediately, the caddy handed him his putter and said, "And now for one heck of a putt!"

❖

A terribly slow-playing golfer was getting heat from his caddy all afternoon when he finally lost his cool. "I've had enough of your snide remarks. When we get back to the clubhouse, I'll see that you no longer have any work here."
"You gotta be kidding," said the caddy. "By the time we get there, I'll be retired."

QUICK QUIZ

In 1979, who became the first player known to score lower than his age, shooting a 66 at the Quad Cities Open at the age of 67?

Sam Snead

Gary Player and Tiger Woods were playing the 14th hole when Tiger's tee shot landed behind a huge 75-foot sycamore tree. Tiger looked at Gary and said, "How would you play this one? Lay up and take an extra stroke?"

Player replied, "When I was your age, I'd just play right over the tree."

Tiger, not wanting to be shown up by the old master, proceeded to hit the ball high, but not high enough. It bounced off the tree and dropped out of bounds. Tiger, really ticked at this point, asked, "Gary, how did you ever hit a ball over that tree?"

Player replied, "Well, when I was your age, that tree was only three feet tall."

❖

Tom runs excitedly into the locker room and holds up a golf ball. "Look at this!" he says.

"Looks like a plain old golf ball to me," says Steve.

"This is no ordinary golf ball," Tom responds. "This is a golf ball that can not be lost."

Steve says, "Yeah, sure. Any ball can be lost."

"Not this one," replies Tom. "It's got a special radar tracking device so that if you hit it into the woods or rough or even the water, you can locate it."

"Oh yeah? Where'd you get this super-duper ball, anyway?"

"I found it."

CHIP SHOT

The first British Open was originally called a "General Golf Tournament for Scotland" and was "open" to only eight invited professionals. It was played at Prestwick in 1860.

Rex had a particularly bad day on the course. Nothing went right, and by the time he missed a two-foot putt on the 17th to round his score up to 130, he blew his stack. He removed his golf clubs from his bag and cracked them over his knees before hurling them into the water.

"I'll never play golf again," he roared. He then kicked the bag around, tossed that in the water too, and in a super-human burst of rage, flipped the golf cart over into the lake. At that point, he stomped off toward the clubhouse.

One of the members happened by, just missing the tantrum, and innocently asked, "Hey Rex, we need a fourth for tomorrow. Can you make it?"

Rex stopped in his tracks, looked up and said, "What time?"

❖

A duffer walks into the 19th hole, orders three stiff ones and downs them immediately, then starts sobbing uncontrollably. The bartender says, "Hey, buddy, calm down. What's the matter?"

"My wife just left me for my golfing partner," he sobs.

"That's okay. Take it easy. There are plenty of other fish in the sea," says the bartender.

"I'm not worried about that," the duffer cries, "but he's the only one I could ever beat."

Quick Quiz

Baseball's all-time career batting leader was a member of Augusta National. Name him.

Ty Cobb

A real fire-and-brimstone fundamentalist preacher always made it a point to admonish his flock about playing golf on the Sabbath. But, alas, one springtime Sunday morning, the preacher himself was tempted to play a quick round. Up in Heaven, the angel in charge of such things, Melrose, spotted the minister and was outraged at his hypocrisy. Melrose went to see the Big Guy and told him of the reverend's transgression.

"I agree he should be punished," said God. "I'll take care of it."

With that, back down on the course, the preacher stepped up to the tee and hit the ball perfectly. It sailed down the fairway, cleared all the hazards, plopped down on the green and rolled gently into the cup for an ace. Melrose was flabbergasted.

"A hole-in-one? I thought you were going to punish him."

"I did," God replied. "Who's he going to tell?"

❖

Barney spent a lot more time on the links than he did in church. In fact, just about the only time he did attend was at a wedding or funeral. And if you didn't know him, you could always tell which one was Barney sitting in the pew. He was the one praying with the interlocking grip.

CHIP SHOT

Against odds of 8,675,083-to-1, four golfers aced the 167-yard 6th hole at Oak Hill in Rochester, New York, during the same round of the 1989 U.S. Open: Mark Wiebe, Jerry Pate, Nick Price, and Doug Weaver.

The drill sergeant decides to play a late afternoon-early evening game of golf and hooks up to play a twosome.

Four quadruple bogeys, three triple bogeys and two double bogeys later the sarge's partner says, "When did you take up this game?"

The drill sergeant says, "Nineteen fifty-nine."

"Nineteen fifty-nine?" says the other golfer. "I would think you'd be able to play a little better than this."

"Whaddya mean?" says the sarge. "It's only twenty-two thirteen right now."

❖

Father Flanagan was playing golf with a parishioner. On the first hole, he sliced his tee shot into the rough. His playing partner heard the priest mutter "Hoover" under his breath.

On the second hole, his ball went straight into a water hazard. Again, the priest muttered, "Hoover."

He got lucky on the third hole as his tee shot landed on the green. "Praise be to God," exclaimed Father Flanagan.

He lined up his five-foot putt but missed it. "Hoover!" he yelled.

His opponent, now curious about the term, asked why the priest said "Hoover."

Father Flanagan responded, "It's the biggest dam I know."

QUICK QUIZ

What kind of object is the British Open trophy?

A claret jug

Gus was keeping score and asked Wilbur what he shot as they finished the sixth hole.

"A 14," said Wilbur.

"What- a 14?!" said Gus incredulously. "How did you ever manage a 14 on a par-3?"

"I sank a 35-foot putt."

❖

Doctor Dudley, toting his golf bag, was heading out of his dentist's office when his receptionist said,"Doctor, I have Mr. Arnold on the line. He has a toothache."

Dudley answered, "Tell him to call back tomorrow. I've got 18 cavities to fill today."

❖

Sheldon's tee shot resulted in a horrible slice that flew over into the next fairway, conking a bystander in the head and knocking him cold. By the time he and his partner Wally arrived, the man was lying unconscious on the ground with the ball between his feet.

"What should I do?" Sheldon blurted out in a panic.

"Don't touch him," said Wally. "If we leave him here, he becomes an immovable obstruction and you can drop the ball two club lengths away."

CHIP SHOT

Walter Diets scored his first hole-in-one on a course near Los Angeles in 1987. What makes it so unusual is that he was blind. Walter had played the course for years when he could see, but it wasn't until his first time out without vision that he shot an ace.

Two old buddies were out on the links on a scorching Wednesday afternoon. On the fifth hole, the first old duffer collapses right on the green. His buddy shouts for help.

A pair of doctors playing the fourth hole quickly drive their cart over. One takes out his emergency kit, examines the old guy and says, "I'm sorry, but your friend is dead."

"He was in perfect condition," said the oldster. "That just can't be. I want a second opinion."

With that, the second doctor goes back to his cart, takes out a small cat from his golf bag, and places it near the dead man. The cat sniffs around the man's feet, walks around his body, and then sits down and begins meowing at the doctor.

"What's that supposed to mean?" asks the old duffer.

"The cat says your friend is dead," responds the doctor.

The man tearfully says, "I can't believe it."

"That'll be $350," says the doctor.

"What? I would agree to pay something, but where do you get off charging me 350 bucks?"

"It's $50 for the diagnosis," replies the doctor, "and $300 for the cat scan."

❖

QUICK QUIZ

Who's the only man with a last name beginning with "Z" to win a major?

Fuzzy Zoeller

87-year-old Mortie, an avid golfer, went to play at the new country club for the first time. Since no one was available to pair up with him, the country club's pro volunteered his services. They decided to make a friendly wager and the pro asked Mortie how many strokes he wanted.

The octogenarian replied, "Oh, I won't need any strokes. My game's been really consistent. I'm just having a tough time getting out of the sand traps." Mortie was true to form. He and the pro were all even when they came to the 18th. The pro had a good drive, was on the green in 2, and 2-putted the par 4 hole. Mortie's drive equaled the pro's, but his approach shot landed in a sand trap next to the green. From the bunker, Mortie then lifted a ball which landed on the green and rolled right into the cup for the birdie, the match, and the bet!

The pro walked over to Mortie and said, "Great shot! Say, I thought you claimed that you had a problem getting out of sand traps?"

"I do," Mortie said. "Could you please give me a hand?"

❖

And then there's the one about the golfer who was so bad that in order to keep from going broke he had to start return addressing the ball.

Chip Shot

The Augusta GreenJackets baseball team, named in honor of the award given to the Masters winner, are a minor league affiliate of the San Francisco Giants.

Duffer-nitions

Graphite Shaft- what the guy who cheats on the scorecard gives you

Green- an area of smooth grass kept verdant and lush from years of constant sprinkling– usually by means of sobbing, whimpering and crying

Foursome- the best way to make slowpokes let you play through

19th Hole- the only place related to the course where players don't worry about how many shots they take

Greenskeeper- the guy at the pro shop who keeps all your money

Driving range- what you want to make sure the hospital is within before playing golf with Charles Barkley

Dogleg- what you'll often see just before a water hazard

Fairway- that unfamiliar tract of closely cropped grass running from the tee to the green– otherwise known as that place your ball usually isn't

Duffer- a golfer whose actual score on any given hole is usually double his or her reported tally

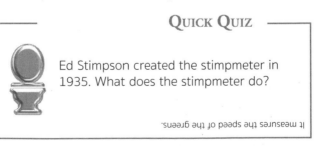

QUICK QUIZ

Ed Stimpson created the stimpmeter in 1935. What does the stimpmeter do?

It measures the speed of the greens.

"Be honest," Weinstein said to his caddy as he teed up his ball on the 18th hole. "Do you see any change in my game since we started?"

The caddy stroked his chin thoughtfully for a moment and replied, "Well sir, they're getting longer."

"My drives?" asked Weinstein.

"No, sir... our shadows."

❖

Barney's on the 18th hole with two golf balls left, an old one and a new one. His tee shot has to go over a lake and he can't make up his mind which ball to play.

All of the sudden, the clouds part and a heavenly voice bellows, "Have faith. Play the new ball."

Barney can't believe his ears, but he's not about to doubt what he just heard, so he tees up the new ball. Once again, a voice from above roars, "Take a practice swing."

Barney scratches his head, but going along with the divine advice, takes his usual hacker's swing. Just as he's about to hit the ball, the clouds part one more time and the voice says, "Play the old ball!"

❖

Chip Shot

Despite losing an eye in World War I, Tommy Armour still won three major titles: the U.S. Open in 1927, the PGA Championship in 1930, and the British Open in 1931.

A very attractive but ill-intended young woman made it a practice to hang around the exclusive country club, looking to settle down with a very rich and very old man. She found one in J.P. Fotheringham, the 92-year-old financier. Sure enough, she and J.P. tied the knot.

Within months, J.P. became ill. As his condition worsened, the old duffer was advised to make a new will. He asked his wife, "Honey, what should I do about my estate?"

She gently hugged him and cooed, "J.P., I think you should leave all of your worldly possessions to your greatest source of comfort."

Just a few days after his rewritten will was made, the old man died. At the reading of his will, his wife learned that he left $20 million to his country club.

❖

Sam and Moe were rocking on the porch of the palatial Miami Country Club after enjoying a round of golf.

Having talked about everything under the sun during their many games together, Sam was grasping for a new topic of conversation.

"Tell me, Moe, have you read Marx?" Sam asked.

"Why, yes," replied Moe. "And you know, I think it's the wicker chairs."

Irving and Irma were a loving, but very competitive couple. They also both talked in their sleep. Irving loved golf and Irma loved auctions. One night, in the wee small hours, Irving cried out, "Fore!"
Irma, deep in slumber, snorted and yelled, "Four-fifty!"

❖

Barry was going by a large and deep bunker when he heard muffled cries for help. Peering down into the trap, he saw his buddy Larry trapped under an overturned golf cart.
"I think my leg is broken," groaned Larry.
"Does our lawyer know you're here?" called Barry.
"No, nobody does."
"Great," said Barry, climbing down into the trap. "Move over."

❖

Abe's ball landed in a deep ravine and as he flailed away trying to get it out, his golfing buddies heard "Whack! Whack! Whack! Whack! Whack! Whack!"
"Say Abe," his friend said when he finally emerged from the ravine, "just how many strokes was that?"
"Three," replied Abe.
"But we heard six."
Abe replied, "Three of them were echoes."

CHIP SHOT

The first time galleries were kept off the fairways and behind ropes at a tournament was in 1954 at the U.S. Open at Baltusrol Golf Club.

Harry the hacker was teeing off on the 16th hole of Pinehurst when he died of a sudden heart attack. The next thing you know, he stood before St. Peter at the Pearly Gates.

"Welcome to heaven, Harry," said St. Peter. "Come, let me show you around the place."

St. Peter led Harry to a variety of beautiful places, including some of the best golf courses he'd ever laid eyes on. At one point, St. Peter brought Harry into a gigantic room with clocks all over the walls.

"What are all these clocks for?" asked Harry.

St. Peter replied, "Ah, these are actually profanity dial indicators for all the golfers who've joined us this year. The more a golfer cussed on the links, the faster the hands move."

"Wow," said Harry. "Where's mine?"

"Sorry to report that they're using yours as a fan for the family room."

❖

Bentley took a series of giant steps as he stepped out of the cart and made his way to the first green.

"What the heck was that all about?" questioned his partner.

"Well," answered Bentley, "my wife told me that if I want to play tomorrow, it'll be over her dead body, so I'm practicing."

QUICK QUIZ

Can you name the golfer who was the first to break 70 in all four rounds of a major championship? (Hint: The year was 1964.)

Arnold Palmer, who shot a 68, 68, 69 and 69 at the PGA championship that year.

Waiting to tee off, an Atlanta gentleman spotted a funeral procession going down a nearby road. It was led by a man walking a dog, followed by the hearse and about 75 to 80 men in single file. As they passed by, the golfer bowed his head and then asked the man about the strange procession.

"Well, suh," drawled the man, "you see, this is my wife's funeral and she died because this dog bit her."

"I'm terribly sorry for your loss," responded the golfer, "but would you mind if I borrowed the dog for a while?"

"Sure," said the widower. "Get in the back of the line."

❖

A duffer sliced his tee shot right into the woods. Rather than take a penalty, he decided to go for it. Unfortunately, his second shot caromed right off the trunk of a big old oak tree, hitting him right between the eyes and killing him instantly.

The next thing he knew, he was standing before St. Peter at the Pearly Gates.

St. Peter, trying to find his name on the list, said, "Oh, here it is. But according to this, you're not scheduled to die for another 25 years. How did you get here?"

"In two."

CHIP SHOT

The Masters was the first major to switch from an 18-hole playoff to sudden death, making the change in 1976.

The Sheik of all sheiks was rushed to the hospital for an emergency appendectomy. The attending surgeon expertly removed the organ without serious complications.

"You saved my life," said the Sheik upon regaining consciousness. "Anything you want is yours."

"That's not necessary," responded the doctor.

"But I insist," said the Sheik.

"Well, okay, I could use a new set of matched clubs."

"Done!" said the Sheik.

A few weeks went by and the busy doctor had forgotten all about the Sheik's promise when an email arrived. It read:

To: The Good Doctor

I have bought you the new set of golf clubs you requested, but am eternally embarrassed and humbled that they sadly do not match. I was appalled to discover that four do not have swimming pools.

The Sheik

❖

Did you hear the one about the pub for vulgar golfers?
It's called Par for the Coarse.

QUICK QUIZ

The first Puerto Rican to be inducted into the World Golf Hall of Fame never won a major in his career. Who is he?

Chi Chi Rodríguez

The Back Nine

A Round of Quotes

"Even when times were good, I realized that my earning power as a golf professional depended on too many ifs and putts." -Gene Sarazen

❖

"I don't even drive that far when I go on vacation." -Raymond Floyd, on John Daly's driving prowess

❖

"I call my sand wedge my half-Nelson, because I can always strangle the opposition with it." -Byron Nelson

---

CHIP SHOT

In 1457, golf was outlawed in Scotland because the lawmakers felt that time spent on the game would be better invested in archery practice to defend Scotland from the English. Guess they didn't realize most golfers could take somebody out faster with a golf ball than an arrow.

"Mulligan: invented by an Irishman who wanted to hit one more 20-yard grounder." -Jim Bishop, writer

❖

"When I make a bad shot, your job is to take the blame." -Seve Ballesteros, to his caddy

❖

"When a pro hits it left to right, it's called a fade. When an amateur hits it left to right, it's called a slice." -Peter Jacobsen

❖

"The worst club in my bag is my brain." -Chris Perry

❖

"I don't know why that putt hung on the edge. I'm a clean liver. It must be my caddie." -JoAnne Carner

❖

"Golf is based on honesty. Where else would someone admit to a seven on an easy par-three?" -Jimmy Demaret

❖

"Give me a man with big hands, big feet, and no brains and I will make a golfer out of him." -Walter Hagen

QUICK QUIZ

With 18, who holds the record for the most PGA tournaments won in a single year?

Byron Nelson, in 1945

"I find it to be the hole-in-one."
-Groucho Marx, on golf's toughest shot

❖

"Putting and dancing are the two things I hate
most." -President George W. Bush

❖

"It took me 17 years to get 3,000 hits. I did it in one
afternoon on the golf course."
-Hank Aaron, baseball Hall of Famer

❖

"I don't have any handicap. I am all handicap."
-President Lyndon B. Johnson

❖

"Never have so many spent so much to sit in relative
comfort to brag about their failures." -Keith Jackson

❖

"Golf is more fun than walking naked in a strange
place, but not much." -Buddy Hackett

❖

"Being left-handed is a big advantage. No one knows
enough about your swing to mess you up with
advice." -Bob Charles

CHIP SHOT

The 1965 U.S. Open was the first to be played
in a four-day format of 18 holes each day.
Before that, golfers played 18 holes the first
two days and a 36-hole final day.

"My putting is so bad I could putt it off a tabletop and leave it short, halfway down a leg." -J.C. Snead

❖

"I've heard it's boring to play golf 365 days a year, but I'd like to find out for myself." -Bob Newhart

❖

"Lay off for three weeks and then quit for good."
-Sam Snead, giving advice to a pupil

❖

"Ninety percent of the putts that fall short don't go in." -Yogi Berra

❖

"I know I'm getting better at golf because I'm hitting fewer spectators." -President Gerald Ford

❖

"I'd do better if the ball were two feet off the ground and moving." -Stan Musial, baseball Hall of Famer

❖

"I'm working as hard as I can to get my life and my cash to run out at the same time. If I can just die after lunch Tuesday, everything will be fine."
-Doug Sanders

QUICK QUIZ

Golf hadn't been an Olympic sport since 1904 before it was revived in 2016. Can you name the men and women's gold medal winners in 2016?

Justin Rose of Great Britain and Korea's Inbee Park

"My best score ever is 103. But I've only been playing 15 years." -Alex Karras

❖

"If you think it's hard to meet new people, try picking up the wrong golf ball." -Jack Lemmon

❖

"The food at this restaurant is like Jack Nicklaus. Very good, and very slow." -Roberto de Vicenzo

❖

"I can airmail the golf ball, but sometimes I don't put the right address on it." -Jim Dent

❖

"I really enjoy doing corporate outings because there are no cuts and I'm low pro every day."
-Dave Stockton

❖

"For most amateurs, the best wood in the bag is the pencil." -Chi Chi Rodriquez

❖

"Don't blame me. Blame the foursome ahead of me." -Lawrence Taylor, on why he was late for football practice

CHIP SHOT

In 1946, Byron Nelson was in the hunt for his second U.S. Open title when his caddy lost his balance and kicked Nelson's ball. That cost Nelson a penalty stroke which would come back to haunt him. He eventually lost the title in a three-way playoff.

"Golf's not that hard. The ball doesn't move."
-Ted Williams, baseball Hall of Famer

❖

"I'm hitting the woods just great, but I'm having a terrible time getting out of them." -Harry Toscano

❖

"I have three-putted in over 40 countries."
-Fred Corcoran

❖

"The only time I talk on a golf course is to my caddie -and only then to complain." -Seve Ballesteros

❖

"I didn't need to finish college to know what golf was all about. All you need to know is to hit the ball, find it and hit again until it disappears into the hole in the ground." -Fuzzy Zoeller

❖

"Winged Foot has the toughest 18 finishing holes in golf." -Dave Marr

❖

"I don't like to watch golf on television. I can't stand whispering." -David Brenner

QUICK QUIZ

The famous Road Hole is the 17th hole at what course?

St. Andrews

"Even the men's room has a double dogleg."
-Dave Stockton, on the Poppy Hills Golf Course

❖

"If it wasn't for golf, I'd probably be a caddy today."
-George Archer

❖

"I was three over- one over a house, one over a patio, and one over a swimming pool."
-George Brett, baseball Hall of Fame

❖

"I have a tip that can take five strokes off anyone's golf game. It's called an eraser." -Arnold Palmer

❖

"I lead the tour in hitting other fairways."
-Joey Sindelar

❖

"You don't necessarily have to bring your clubs to play golf - just lie about your score."
-Lon Simmons, announcer

❖

"Golf isn't a sport; it's men in ugly pants walking."
-Rosie O'Donnell

CHIP SHOT

On a hot summer day at the 1986 Anheuser Busch Golf Classic, Bill Kratzert managed to lose three balls during play and had to withdraw from the event because he ran out of them. His caddie, trying to lighten the golf bag, didn't bring any extra ones!

"If there's anything to this astrology business, Jack Nicklaus must have been born under every sign."
-Gibby Gilbert

❖

"I drew a big gallery today. I was paired with Arnold Palmer." -Gene Littler

❖

"How did I four-putt? I missed the hole. I missed the hole. I missed the hole. I made it." -Fuzzy Zoeller

❖

"I tell myself that Jack Nicklaus probably has a lousy curve ball." -Bob Walk, former Major League pitcher

❖

"The safest place would be on the fairway."
-Joe Garagiola, on where to stand at a celebrity tournament

❖

"I'm not an intellectual person. I don't get headaches from concentration. I get them from double bogeys." -Tom Weiskopf

❖

"There are no straight lines on my courses. The good Lord never drew a straight line." -Jack Nicklaus

---

QUICK QUIZ

What color sweater does the winner of the Arnold Palmer Invitational receive?

Red

"Columbus went around the world in 1492. That isn't a lot of strokes when you consider the course."
-Lee Trevino

❖

"The putter is a club designed to hit the ball partway to the hole." -Rex Lardner, humorist

❖

"Most people retire to play golf and fish. I do that now." -Julius Boros, on his reluctance to retire

❖

"The way I hit the ball today, I need to go to the range. Instead, I think I'll go to the bar."
-Fuzzy Zoeller

❖

"I play in the low 80s. If it's any hotter than that, I won't play." -Joe E. Lewis, comedian

❖

"A cardinal rule for the club breaker is never to break your putter and driver in the same match or you are dead." -Tommy Bolt

❖

"That's a bagful of indecision." -Jack Burke, when Arnold Palmer brought eight putters to a tournament

Chip Shot

"Do you believe in miracles?!" That famous line made by Al Michaels to describe the 1980 U.S. Olympic hockey team's win over the Soviet Union is used by the sportscaster to this day. Michaels admits, "It's usually on the golf course after a long birdie putt."

"The way I putted, I must have been reading the greens in Spanish and putting them in English."
-Homero Blancas

❖

"The number one thing about trouble is: Don't get into more!" -Dave Stockton

❖

"How do I address the ball? I say, 'Hello there, ball. Are you going to go in the hole or not?'" -Flip Wilson

❖

"My swing is no uglier than Arnold Palmer's, and it's the same ugly swing every time." -Nancy Lopez

❖

"I'll get up at five in the morning to do only two things: go to the bathroom and play golf."
-Jim McMahon, former NFL quarterback

❖

"Some guys hope to shoot their age. Craig Stadler hopes to shoot his waist." -Jim Murray, writer

❖

"My turn-ons? Big galleries, small scores, long drives, short rough, fat paychecks, and skinny trees."
-Peter Jacobsen

QUICK QUIZ

What course's seventh hole features "Hell's Half Acre", one of the golf world's largest hazards?

Pine Valley

"It's hard to take a chance when you can't reach the green in the first place." -Tom Kite

❖

"I'll take a two-shot penalty, but I'll be damned if I'm going to play the ball where it lies." -Elaine Johnson, after her shot hit a tree and caromed into her bra

❖

"Golf is a game in which the ball lies poorly and the players well." -Art Rosenblum, comedian

❖

"Man blames fate for other accidents, but feels personally responsible for a hole-in-one."
-Martha Beckman

❖

"I only hit the ball about 220 off the tee, but I can always find it." -Bonnie Lauer

❖

"The rest of the field."
-Roger Maltbie, on what he had to shoot to win

❖

"I paid my dues. That's golfer-talk for hitting a million balls." -Jim Thorpe

CHIP SHOT

Up until 1982, golfers were assigned local caddies for The Masters and were not allowed to bring their own.

"Real golfers have two handicaps: one for braggin'
and one for bettin'." -Anonymous

❖

"I never thought I'd live to shoot my age. I thought
somebody would shoot me first." -Dale Morey

❖

"I've seen better swings on a condemned
playground." -Arnold Palmer, to Bob Hope

❖

"Did you know that John Daly hit a tee shot - and
two tracking stations picked it up as a satellite?"
-Jim Murray

❖

"The trouble with golf is you're only as good as your
last putt." -Doug Sanders

❖

"I never wanted to be a millionaire. I just wanted to
live like one." -Walter Hagen

❖

"Short putts test the character of the golfer. Long
putts test the patience of the other golfers in his
foursome." -Anonymous

QUICK QUIZ

You're on the first tee, ready to make your
first shot of the day. What's the ruling if
you accidentally knock the ball off the tee
at address?

No stroke, so no penalty. Tee it up again.

"If I'da cleared the trees and drove the green, it would'a been a great tee shot." -Sam Snead

❖

"I've heard of unplayable lies, but on the tee?" -Bob Hope

❖

"You drive for show and putt for dough." -Al Balding

❖

"Heck, I wish they'd make the gallery ropes out of bounds. We're the only sport that plays in the audience." -Lee Trevino

❖

"I'm so busy I can only play in one tournament at a time." -Jack Nicklaus

❖

"I'm allergic to grass. Hey, it could be worse. I could be allergic to beer." -Greg Norman

❖

"The only thing worse than missing a cut is missing a cut and staying in the same town. That's torture. That's like staying at the scene of the crime." -Joey Sindelar

Chip Shot

The largest collection of golf books in the world belongs to the USGA Museum and Library, which has a collection of golf magazines dating back to 1880.

"I own all the erasers for all the miniature golf pencils." -Steven Wright

❖

"Hold up a one-iron and walk. Even God can't hit a one-iron." -Lee Trevino, on how to deal with lightning

❖

"The Senior Tour is like a class reunion. It's the same as it was 30 years ago. We tell the same dirty jokes- only they're funnier now." -Bob Toski

❖

"Golf is a game in which you yell 'fore', shoot six, and write down five." -Paul Harvey

❖

"Anyone who criticizes a golf course is like a person invited to a house for dinner who, on leaving, tells the host that the food was lousy." -Gary Player

❖

"Every driver has its own personality. I am looking for one that matches my own." -Morris Hatalsky

❖

"I'd like to see the fairways more narrow. Then everybody would have to play from the rough, not just me." -Seve Ballesteros

QUICK QUIZ

Stroke of Genius is a 2004 film based on the golfing career of the first player to win all four men's major golf championships consecutively. Who?

Bobby Jones

"Swing hard in case you hit it." -Dan Marino

❖

"Every time I have the urge to play golf I lie down until the urge passes." -Sam Levenson, humorist

❖

"You can talk to a fade, but a hook won't listen."
-Lee Trevino

❖

"I played so bad, I got a get well card from the IRS."
-Johnny Miller, on his bad year

❖

"I deny allegations by Bob Hope that during my last game I hit an eagle, a birdie, an elk, and a moose."
-Gerald Ford

❖

"Never bet with anyone you meet on the first tee who has a deep suntan, a one-iron in his bag, and squinty eyes." -Dave Marr

❖

"Golf is easier than catching, but there's nothing easy about finding my ball."
-Johnny Bench, Hall of Fame catcher

CHIP SHOT

At Uganda's Jinja Golf Course, you must let elephants play through- they have the right of way.

"I wish my name was Tom Kite."
-Ian Baker-Finch, on signing autographs

❖

"I used to shoot my age. Now I would just like to
shoot my temperature." -Jerry Feliciotto

❖

"If you drink, don't drive. Don't even putt."
-Dean Martin

❖

"Arnold Palmer is the biggest crowd pleaser since
the invention of the portable sanitary facility."
-Bob Hope

❖

"Sometimes I think that the only way the Spanish
people will recognize me is if I win the Grand Slam
and then drop dead on the 18th green."
-Seve Ballesteros

❖

"Golf got complicated when I had to wear shoes and
begin thinking about what I was doing." -Sam Snead

❖

"The secret of missing a tree is to aim straight at it."
-Michael Green

QUICK QUIZ

What golf Hall of Famer is credited with
inventing the sand wedge?

Gene Sarazen

"If you can't break 80, you have no business playing golf. If you can break 80, you have no business."
-British adage

❖

"He hits it into the woods so often he should get an orange hunting jacket."
-Tom Weiskopf, on then-rookie Ben Crenshaw

❖

"He married the first girl who'd shag balls for him."
-George Low, on Arnold Palmer

❖

"When Jack Nicklaus plays well, he wins. When he plays badly, he finishes second. When he plays terribly, he finishes third." -Johnny Miller

❖

"I hit two fairways - well, maybe four, but only two I was aiming at." -John Daly

❖

"Golf Pro: An optimistic doctor who has a cure for dying." -Jim Bishop, writer

❖

"You've just one problem. You stand too close to the ball - after you've hit it." -Sam Snead, to a pupil

CHIP SHOT

Former president George W. Bush and future wife Laura spent their first date at a miniature golf course.

"Peter Jacobsen is in a position where a birdie will help him more than a bogey."
-Steve Melnyk, announcer, at the 1983 Colonial

❖

"It's a marriage. If I had to choose between my wife and my putter, well, I'd miss her." -Gary Player

❖

"I had a wonderful experience on the golf course today. I had a hole in nothing. Missed the ball and sank the divot." -Don Adams

❖

"Seve Ballesteros drives the ball into territory Daniel Boone couldn't find." -Fuzzy Zoeller

"I don't mind it when I hit a ball into the woods. I think of it as an adventure." -Michelle Wie

❖

"I never did see the sense in keeping my head down. The only reason I play golf at all is to see where the ball goes." -Charles Price, writer

❖

"It's a lot easier hitting a quarterback than a little white ball." -Bubba Smith, former football player

QUICK QUIZ

Tiger Woods is far and away tops on the PGA Tour in money winnings. Who is second?

Phil Mickelson

"My handicap? Arthritis." -Bobby Jones

❖

"My game is impossible to help. Ben Hogan said every time he gave me a lesson it added two shots to his game." -Phil Harris, comedian

❖

"I know I haven't won a lot of tournaments, but my banker doesn't know the difference." -Payne Stewart

❖

"Jerry Pate withdrew citing a shoulder injury, and Jack Renner withdrew citing his score."
-John Morris, USGA official

❖

"Some hotel rugs are impossible to putt."
-Tom Watson

❖

"Hell, I don't need to know where the green is. Where is the golf course?"
-Babe Ruth, playing Pine Valley

❖

"Jack Nicklaus has become a legend in his spare time." -Chi Chi Rodriguez

---

CHIP SHOT

Winless in 18 years on the PGA Tour, Gary McCord had "NO WINS" inscribed on his vanity license plate. When he finally won on the Hogan Tour in 1991, McCord added an asterisk to the plate.

"The toughest hole is the 19th. I just can't get through it. It takes the longest time to play."
-Craig Stadler

❖

"My car absolutely will not run unless my golf clubs are in the trunk." -Bruce Berlet, writer

❖

"The first time Bob Gibson ever let himself get talked into a celebrity golf tournament, he shot a score of 115. It was his own fault. He counted all his strokes."
-Bob Uecker, baseball announcer

❖

"The sand was heavier than I thought and it only took me four swings to figure it out." -Johnny Miller

❖

"My putter will not be flying first-class home with me." -Nick Faldo

❖

"I don't say my golf game is bad; but if I grew tomatoes, they'd come up sliced." -Miller Barber

❖

"Now I can see I can't make anything."
-Jack Nicklaus, on his new contact lenses

QUICK QUIZ

Who holds the record for appearing in the most Masters?

Sam Snead, 44

"Gary Player solicits far too much advice on the practice tee. I've seen him taking a lesson at the U.S. Open from a hot dog vendor." -Dave Hill

❖

"How did I take a 12? I had a long putt for an 11." -Clayton Heafner

❖

"I'm not concerned about getting in the record books. A good obituary doesn't exactly excite me." -JoAnne Carner

❖

"I've never been to Heaven and thinkin' back on my life, I probably won't get a chance to go. I guess The Masters is as close as I'm going to get." -Fuzzy Zoeller

❖

"That hasn't been Johnny Miller out there. That's been somebody else with somebody else's swing." -Johnny Miller, in a slump

❖

"Sam is so loose that if you cut his wrist, 3-in-1 Oil would come out." -Gardner Dickinson, on Sam Snead

---

CHIP SHOT

The maiden name of Jack Nicklaus's wife is Barbara Bush.

"It's like playing in a straitjacket. They just lay you up on the rack and twist on both ends."
-Ben Crenshaw, on U.S. Open pressure

❖

"If I had known it was going in the water, I wouldn't have hit it there." -Mike Reid

❖

"Belly dancers would make great golfers. They never move their heads." -Phil Rodgers

❖

"I don't make mistakes. I make disasters."
-Bob Goalby

❖

"I'm very even-tempered on the golf course. I stay mad all the time." -Bob Murphy

❖

"You can play a damned good shot there and find the ball in a damned bad place." -George Duncan, British Open champ, on St Andrews

❖

"At my age, I don't even buy green bananas."
-Lee Trevino, 47, at the 1987 British Open

QUICK QUIZ

Which major is the first one played in the calendar year?

The Masters (April)

"My IQ must be two points lower than a plant's."
-Tom Watson, explaining his disqualification for
illegally changing putters

❖

"What's nice about our Tour is you can't remember
your bad shots."
-Bobby Brue, on the Senior PGA Tour

❖

"I learn English from American professionals…
That's why I speak so bad. I call it PGA English."
-Roberto De Vicenzo

❖

"Like a lot of fellows around here, I have a furniture
problem. My chest has fallen into my drawers."
-Billy Casper, on the Senior PGA Tour

❖

"When I was younger, I was 'an angry player'. Now
all of a sudden I'm a 'fiery competitor.' I like the
change in vocabulary." -Corey Pavin

❖

"Man, I go rabbit hunting in that stuff. You don't go
in there; you send your beagle in there to get
something out."
-Fuzzy Zoeller, on the rough at Shinnecock Hills

CHIP SHOT

JoAnn Washam is the only golfer to ace two
holes in the same LPGA tournament. Washam
did it in the second and final rounds of the
1979 Women's Kemper Open.

"I couldn't read the break in the green from the tee."
-Gary Player, after just missing a hole-in-one

❖

"Hubert Green's swing looks like a drunk trying to
find a keyhole in the dark." -Jim Murray, writer

❖

"If you want to beat somebody on the golf course,
just get him mad." -Dave Williams

❖

"Bad sausage and five bogeys will give you a
stomach ache every time." -Miller Barber

❖

"You have to put your putter out to pasture every so
often, let it eat and get fat so it can get more birdies."
-Greg Norman

❖

"The reason the Road Hole at St Andrews is the
most difficult par-4 in the world is that it was
designed as a par-6." -Ben Crenshaw

❖

"He's playing a game I'm not familiar with. Of
course, I'm playing a game I'm not familiar with."
-Jack Nicklaus, on Tiger Woods

QUICK QUIZ

What Pennsylvania golf course became a
National Historic Landmark in 1987?

Oakmont

"These greens are so fast, I have to hold my putter over the ball and hit it with the shadow." -Sam Snead

❖

"My luck is so bad that if I bought a cemetery, people would stop dying."
-Ed Furgol, 1954 U.S. Open champion

❖

"I don't care to join any club that's prepared to have me as a member." -Groucho Marx

❖

"Be funny on a golf course? Do I kid my best friend's mother about her heart condition?"
-Phil Silvers, comedian

❖

"The golf swing is like sex in this respect. You can't be thinking about the mechanics of the act while you're performing." -Dave Hill

❖

"She is so small, she might get lost in an un-replaced divot." -Bob Toski, on LPGA player Judy Rankin

❖

"Here, Eddie, hold the flag while I putt out."
-Walter Hagen, to Edward, Prince of Wales

CHIP SHOT

In 1899, golfers at the Atlantic City (N.J.) CC came up with the word "birdie" when George Crump put his second shot inches from the hole on a par four after his ball hit a bird in flight.

"When I ask you what kind of club to use, look the other way and don't answer."
-Sam Snead, to his caddy

❖

"Golf seems to me an arduous way to go for a walk. I prefer to take the dogs out."
-Princess Anne of England

❖

"I don't trust doctors. They are like golfers. Every one has a different answer to your problems."
-Seve Ballesteros

❖

"I regard golf as an expensive way of playing marbles." -G.K. Chesterton, writer

❖

"I've built golf courses and laid the irrigation system just by teeing off." -Lee Trevino

❖

"Is it against the rules to carry a bulldozer in your bag?" -Tom Watson

❖

"A sick appendix is not as difficult to deal with as a five-foot putt." -Gene Sarazen

QUICK QUIZ

He won the U.S. Open in 2017 and 2018, and the PGA Championship in 2018 and 2019, becoming the first golfer to hold back-to-back titles in two majors simultaneously. Who is he?

Brooks Koepka

"Tranquilizers make it possible for a golfer to relax at his favorite form of relaxation."
-Stephen Baker, writer

❖

"The difference between me and an amateur is that I'm not afraid to screw up." -Fuzzy Zoeller

❖

"Usually when I wake up in the middle of the night, it's to do something else." -Tiger Woods, when asked if he ever wakes up at night to think about what he's accomplished in golf

❖

"The only problem with the Senior Tour is that when you're through here, they put you in a box."
-J.C. Snead

❖

"Anything I want it to be. For instance, this hole right here is a par-47, and yesterday I birdied the sucker."
-Willie Nelson, country music singer, when asked what par was on the golf course he owns

❖

"Don't play too much golf. Two rounds a day is plenty." -Harry Vardon

---

CHIP SHOT

Way back when, this sports headline appeared in the *St. Louis Post-Dispatch*:
"Shot Off Woman's Leg Helps Nicklaus to 66."

"I would like to think of myself as an athlete first, but I don't want to do a disservice to the real ones." -David Duval

❖

"You know what I did at The Masters one year? I was so nervous I drank a fifth of rum before I played. I shot the happiest 83 of my life." -Chi Chi Rodriguez

❖

"I'm trying as hard as I can, and sometimes things don't go your way, and that's the way things go." -Tiger Woods

❖

"I could never believe in a game where the person who hits the ball least wins." -Winston Churchill

❖

"I'm the worst golfer in the world and the worst singer in the world and I love both of those. Maybe I should sing while I'm playing golf." -Jamie Farr

❖

"Golf does strange things to other people, too. It makes liars out of honest men, cheats out of altruists, cowards out of brave men, and fools out of everybody." -Milton Gross, writer

QUICK QUIZ

Who famously played the groundskeeper in *Caddyshack* and has also played in quite a few celebrity and charity events?

Bill Murray

"I like to say I was born on the 19th hole- the only one I ever parred." -George Low, former Tour player

❖

"I am the handicap in golf." -Boris Becker, tennis great

❖

"A hundred years of experience has demonstrated that the game is temporary insanity practiced in a pasture." -Dave Kindred, columnist

❖

"Golf, like measles, should be caught young, for if postponed to riper years, the results may be serious." -P.G. Wodehouse, writer

❖

"Golf is not a game of great shots. It's a game of the most accurate misses. The people who win make the smallest mistakes." -Gene Littler

❖

"Golf is the only sport where the object is to play as little as possible." -Charles G. McLaughlin, writer

❖

"The harder you work, the luckier you get." -Gary Player

CHIP SHOT

Lingo of the Links: A "toilet flusher" is a putt that swirls around the rim of the hole.

"If you think the game is just a matter of getting it close and letting the law of averages do your work for you, you'll find a different way to miss every time." -Jack Nicklaus

❖

"Putting is the greatest psychological arena on the golf course and many are the mighty who have fallen there." -Dr. David C. Morley

❖

"Golf is like art. It's impossible to be perfect."
-Sandra Palmer

❖

"The arc of your swing doesn't have a thing to do with the size of your heart." -Carol Mann

❖

"No matter how hard I try, I just can't seem to break 64." -Jack Nicklaus

❖

"Bad golf is played with the shoulders and the body. Good golf is played with the hands." -Gene Sarazen

❖

"Make the hard ones look easy and the easy ones look hard." -Walter Hagen

QUICK QUIZ

What golfers have these nicknames:
The Shark, The Golden Bear, and
The Desert Fox?

Greg Norman, Jack Nicklaus and Johnny Miller, respectively

"If you've got to remind yourself to concentrate during competition, you've got no chance to concentrate." -Bobby Nichols

❖

"Probably I'm a hell of a lot more famous for being the guy who hit the golf ball on the moon than the first guy in space."
-Alan Shepard, Apollo 14 astronaut

❖

"On the golf course, a man may be the dogged victim of inexorable fate, be struck down by an appalling stroke of tragedy, become the hero of unbelievable melodrama, or the clown in a side-splitting comedy." -Bobby Jones

❖

"The difference between golf and the government is that in golf you can't improve your lie."
-George Deukmejian, former California Governor

❖

"The thing with golf is, it's like a cat chasing its tail. You're never going to catch it. The day you think you've got your swing down pat, something goes awry and you've got to go back to the driving range."
-Greg Norman

CHIP SHOT

Tee off at the "Fra Mauro Country Club" and you'll literally be hitting moon shots. That's the name of the lunar landing spot where Alan Shepard played golf.

"Talking to a golf ball won't do you any good- unless you do it while your opponent is teeing off."
-Bruce Lansky, author

❖

"Golf is neither a microcosm of nor a metaphor for life. It is a sport, a bloodless sport, if you don't count ulcers." -Dick Schaap

❖

"I don't care what anybody says. The first tournament is not the hardest one to win. It's always the second one." -John Daly

❖

"Golf is a game invented by God to punish guys who retire early." -Red Green

❖

"The object of a bunker or trap is not only to punish a physical mistake, to punish lack of control, but also to punish pride and egotism."
-Charles Blair MacDonald, writer

❖

"That little white ball won't move until you hit it, and there's nothing you can do after it has gone."
-Babe Zaharias

QUICK QUIZ

Which of the majors is played on the same course every year?

The Masters

"Golf is not a funeral, although both can be very sad affairs." -Bernard Darwin, writer

❖

"The guy who chokes the least wins the most." -Hubert Green

❖

"Relax? How can anybody relax and play golf? You have to grip the club, don't you?" -Ben Hogan

❖

"There's no better game in the world when you are in good company, and no worse game when you are in bad company." -Tommy Bolt

❖

"Baseball players quit playing and they play golf. Football players quit, take up golf. What are we supposed to take up when we quit?" -George Archer

❖

"You can make a lot of money out of golf. Just ask my ex-wives." -Lee Trevino

❖

"Golf was never meant to be an exact science- it's an art form. Einstein was a great scientist but a lousy golfer." -Bob Toski

CHIP SHOT

In 1888, the St. Andrew's GC of Yonkers, N.Y., spent a total of $28.42 for the upkeep of the six-hole golf course.

"I don't know of any game that makes you so
ashamed of your profanity. It is a game full of
moments of self-abasement, with only a few
moments of self-exaltation."
-President William Howard Taft

❖

"The only thing that you should force in a golf swing
is the club back into the bag." -Byron Nelson

❖

"Competitors take bad breaks and use them to drive
themselves just that much harder. Quitters take bad
breaks and use them as reasons to give up."
-Nancy Lopez

❖

"They call it golf because all of the other four-letter
words were taken." -Raymond Floyd

❖

"The biggest liar in the world is the golfer who claims
he plays the game merely for the exercise."
-Tommy Bolt

❖

"Golfers used to check the grass on the greens.
Today they study the roots under the blade."
-Jimmy Demaret

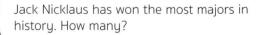

QUICK QUIZ

Jack Nicklaus has won the most majors in
history. How many?

18

"Gentlemen play golf. And if you aren't a gentleman when you start, after the crushing events of the game, you surely become one." -Bing Crosby

❖

"Baseball player, football player, hockey player retires, he takes up golf. I've never heard of a golfer retiring and taking up hockey. This is the greatest game." -Lee Trevino

❖

"Golf is temporary insanity practiced in a pasture." -Dave Kindred, writer

❖

"If you have a bad grip, you don't want a good swing." -Harvey Penick

❖

"I play this game because my sole ambition is to do well enough to give it up." -David Feherty

❖

"Baseball reveals character; golf exposes it." -Ernie Banks, baseball Hall of Famer

❖

"Golf is a game played on a five-inch course between the ears." -Bobby Jones

---

CHIP SHOT

The green jacket was introduced at the 1949 Masters. The first recipient was Sam Snead.

"To really lose weight playing golf, the best place to play is Mexico. Go to any Mexican golf course, stop at every hole and drink water. Within a week you'll be down to your desired weight." -Buddy Hackett

❖

"Golf is a dumb game. Hitting the ball is the fun part of it, but the fewer times you hit the ball, the more fun you have. Does this make any sense?"
-Lou Graham

❖

"Golf combines two favorite American pastimes: taking long walks and hitting things with a stick."
-P.J. O'Rourke, writer

❖

"You can shoot lions in the dark and yet you can quiver like a leaf and fall flat over a two-foot putt."
-Johnny Farrell

❖

"If you pick up a golfer and hold it up to your ear, like a conch shell, you will hear an alibi." -Fred Beck

❖

"I want to win here, stand on the 18th green, and say 'I'm going to the World Series.'"
-Larry Nelson, on a golf tournament in Disney World

QUICK QUIZ

Name the two U.S. presidents who are in the World Golf Hall of Fame.

Dwight Eisenhower and George H.W. Bush

In The Clubhouse

Anecdotes

Ball Fore

Don Zimmer's 65-year career until his death in 2014 was a testament to his pro baseball expertise, a word that could not be used to describe his golf ability. Still in all, Zimmer managed to ace the par-3 12th hole at Wentworth Golf Club in Tarpon Springs, Florida, in 2001. Rather than keep the hole-in-one ball as a souvenir, Zimmer figured it would bring him luck and used it to hit his very next shot- straight into the middle of the pond and out of sight. After winding up with an astronomical 135 for the round, Zimmer said, "The ball brought me luck- just not the right kind."

CHIP SHOT

The Ryder Cup, now played in September, was originally held in June. In 1935, after the British complained of having to play in the heat of Ridgewood, N.J., a plan was worked out to move the match to a cooler month.

One for the Record Books

Former big league baseball player Eric Byrnes set a new world record for speed golf in 2017 when he played 420 holes in a 24-hour span at the Ocean Course at Half Moon Bay Golf Links in California. Byrnes, who spent 11 seasons with five teams and is now an analyst for the MLB Network, is no stranger to feats of endurance. He's been known to run treacherous 100-mile trail races and completed the first-ever transcontinental triathlon in 2016 by swimming seven miles across the San Francisco Bay, biking 2,400 miles from Oakland to Chicago and then running 905 miles from Chicago to New York City. In all, it took 56 days.

Byrnes was 43 years old when he broke the speed golf record previously held by Australian Ian Colston, who hit the 401 hole mark in 1971.

Jack Goes Clubbing

In a fit of road rage, Jack Nicholson once teed off on another driver's car with a golf club because he was cut off in traffic. He later said he was "out of his mind," but admitted he was rational enough to do the bashing with his 2-iron, which he never used on the links.

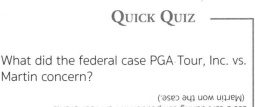

QUICK QUIZ

What did the federal case PGA Tour, Inc. vs. Martin concern?

Whether disabled golfer Casey Martin should be permitted to use a cart during competition in PGA Tour events (Martin won the case.)

A Babe at the Masters

In the history of the four modern men's major championships, the youngest player to ever make the cut is Guan Tianlang of China. He was just 14 years, 5 months and 18 days old when he made it to the weekend in the 2013 Masters and completed the tournament. (Trivia note: Oddly, he's also the last player in Masters history to receive a slow-play penalty stroke.)

By the way, the youngest player to make a cut in any major championship is Michelle Wie, who was 13 years, 5 months and 17 days old when she qualified for the 2003 Kraft Nabisco Championship (now known as the ANA Inspiration).

The POTUS and Links Larceny

According to the 2019 book, *Commander in Cheat: How Golf Explains Trump*, author Rick Reilly says Donald Trump doesn't just cheat at golf. He cheats like a three-card Monte dealer. He throws it, boots it, and moves it. He lies about his lies. He fudges and foozles and fluffs. At Winged Foot, where Trump is a member, the caddies got so used to seeing him kick his ball back onto the fairway they came up with a nickname for him: "Pele."

Chip Shot

Heading for the 19th hole? Experts say if you play a round of golf, then drink two cocktails, you've just gained more calories than you burned.

Potty Picks

When Becky Lucidi was an LPGA Tour rookie in 2007, she wrote a blog about some of the fascinating names she came across on the door of the outdoor portable toilets used on tournament courses.

Her top ten list:

10. Royal Flush
9. Tanks-a-Lot
8. Wizards of Ooze
7. UrinBiz.com
6. Honey Bucket
5. Blue Castle
4. The Drop Zone
3. Oui Oui Enterprises
2. Willy Make It?
1. Doody Calls

Out on a Limb

In 1993, Germany's Bernhard Langer lodged a ball 20 feet up in a tree while playing in a tournament in England. Langer climbed the tree and knocked the ball out. Afterwards, when asked what club he had used, Langer responded, "a tree iron, of course."

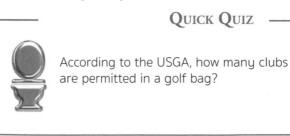

QUICK QUIZ

According to the USGA, how many clubs are permitted in a golf bag?

14

Two for the Ages

Jim Kaat, who won 283 big league games over 25 seasons as a southpaw pitcher, goes both ways as a golfer. And if shooting one's age calls for special recognition, Kaat deserves double the praise. As a lefthanded golfer, Kaat has shot his age or better on numerous occasions. On December 7, 2013, the ambidexterous 75-year-old shot his age playing righthanded, thus becoming the first golfer on record to shoot his age as a lefthander and righthander.

Seinfeld Says

"Golf is the ultimate avoidance activity for the dysfunctional dad- a game so nonsensically difficult, so pointless, so irrationally time consuming- the word golf could only stand for, 'Get out, leave family.' I have a lot of friends that love to play, try to get me to play. All golfers say the same thing to you. 'It's a very challenging game.' I'm sure it is. It's challenging to throw a tic-tac 100 yards into a shoebox. That's not a reason to devote thousands of hours to a game that basically at its highest skill level is, 'Whack! Where is it? Oh, dammit.'"
-Jerry Seinfeld

Chip Shot

The first known women's tournament took place in Scotland in 1810. First prize was a fish basket.

The Bear and the Dog

Jack Nicklaus related this anecdote about a fellow he met at a dinner. The guy claimed his dog loved watching golf on television. He said, "The dog flips head over heels whenever you make a par and flips twice for a birdie."

Nicklaus asked him, "What does the dog do when I win?"

The man shrugged and said, "I don't know. I've only had the dog for five years."

Man Dies on Golf Course, Friends Play Through

Believe it or not, the headline you just read was a real one, albeit a real old one, from an Associated Press release. Officials at a Winter Haven, Florida, golf course covered the golfer's body with a sheet "right where he died, on the 16th green. The body stayed there two hours, while friends and neighbors played through."

"It was a real shock to all of us, but there was nothing we could do," said one of the golfers. "We all thought to ourselves, 'Gee, that's a good way to go.' He didn't suffer."

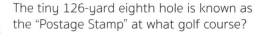

QUICK QUIZ

The tiny 126-yard eighth hole is known as the "Postage Stamp" at what golf course?

Royal Troon

How Could He Miss?
There are Holes in Every Direction!

Alan Shepard became the first extraterrestrial golfer when he retrieved his smuggled 6-iron and package of balls from Apollo XIV in February, 1971, and took some practice shots on the moon. Even his poorest shot in the low gravity, airless environment of the lunar surface soared over 400 yards. As Shepard remarked with some satisfaction, "Not bad for a 6-iron!"

Nantz's Non-Sequitur

Sportscaster Jim Nantz was on the air for a recap of the AT&T Pebble Beach National Pro-Am just after Davis Love had won the event. Joining him was guest celebrity Clint Eastwood.
Nantz thought he'd go ahead and make Clint's day when he remarked to Eastwood, "I'll bet you didn't know that when Davis was a young boy, one of the first adult films his father ever took him to see was one of yours."
Without missing a beat, Eastwood turned to Nantz and said, "I have never made an adult film in my life."

CHIP SHOT

The word "tee" comes from the Scottish term "teay", which is a small pile of sand. In days long gone by, golfers would make a teay and place the ball on top of it for driving.

Who's The Real Goat Here?

At Florida's Sawgrass, Pete Dye got the idea to keep
the weedy under-growth in the rough under control
by using small herds of goats as they do in Ireland.
The idea worked for a short time and then they had
to buy mowers. Pete forgot that Ireland doesn't have
alligators.

Fore!-Head

Mac McLendon wasn't doing very well in the first
round of the 1979 Masters. He was possessed by an
eerie feeling that he was going to hit someone with
one of his shots. That night he shared his fear with
his wife Joan. A good and dutiful wife, she reassured
him and gave him the confidence to go out the next
day. Freed of his apprehensions, he knew he'd play
better. On the first hole, with his very first swing, he
managed to conk a spectator- his wife!

Hookers and Hookers

In 2002, golf tournament organizers in Norco,
California, were arrested after police complained
that prostitutes had been stationed at various areas
on the course and were available to golfers between
holes.

QUICK QUIZ

What golfer, who died in a 1999 airplane
accident, was once sponsored by the
National Football League and wore the
colors and logos of various teams?

Payne Stewart

Ticking Off The Golf Gods

Arnold Palmer lost the 1967 Bing Crosby Pro-Am by virtue of the fact that his tee shot on the 14th at Pebble Beach hit a tree and bounced out of bounds. He re-teed and tried again only to hit the same tree. Late that night, storm clouds gathered and a fierce Pacific gale uprooted the offending tree, ensuring that it would never bother Arnie again.

Presidential Pests

Richard Nixon may have had bugs and leaks, but Dwight Eisenhower had a squirrel problem at the White House. The frisky critters were interfering with his putting practice on the lawn so he ordered them trapped and taken elsewhere. It wasn't as humane as you'd think. After all, where else but Washington, D.C. were the squirrels going to find as many nuts?

Bar for the Course

Back in 1974, during an Amateur Stroke Play event, Nigel Denham hit his second shot right into the clubhouse, winding up in the men's bar. As it wasn't out of bounds, Nigel opened a window and sent the ball to the green, landing just twelve feet from the hole.

CHIP SHOT

Charles Sands of the United States won the first Olympic gold medal in men's golf at the 1900 Paris Olympics.

These Golfers Needed Two Pairs of Socks...Because they got a hole in one.

(Sorry, but we had to fit the world's oldest golf groaner in here somehow.)

53-year-old Sheila Drummond recorded a 144-yard hole-in-one at the Mahoning Valley Country Club, near Lehighton, Pennsylvania, in 2007. Mrs. Drummond is blind.

❖

In 2014, Gus Andreone aced the 113-yard 14th hole at Lakes Course at Palm Aire in Sarasota, Florida. It was Andreone's eighth ace and at 103, he became the oldest golfer to record a hole-in-one.

❖

Dave Ragaini used a 3-wood at a 207 yard, par-3 hole at Wykagyl Country Club at New Rochelle, New York, and hit a hole-in-one. Oh, yes - he was standing on his knees at the time!

❖

On New Year's Eve in 1989 Jenny Ritchie celebrated with a hole-in-one at New Zealand's Wanganui Golf Club. The following day, same place, same story- another ace!

QUICK QUIZ

Your caddy lost your putter. Are you allowed to replace it during the round?

ON

The longest recorded hole-in-one by a woman occurred in 1949 when Marie Robie aced the 393-yard hole at Furnace Brook in Wollaston, MA.

❖

Tiger Woods was six years old when he hit his first hole-in-one. He has 20 altogether. So does Jack Nicklaus, whose last hole-in-one came in a practice round when he was 63.

❖

Amateur Jim Whelehan of Rochester, NY, was playing an 18-hole round in 1992 when he shot a hole-in-one on the fourth hole of the Heather Glen Golf Links in Myrtle Beach, SC. Thrilled by his feat, he decided to play a second round and later that day, same ball, same hole, same result- he aced it once again.

❖

Three U.S. presidents have recorded aces: Dwight Eisenhower, Richard Nixon and Gerald Ford. Nixon said his hole-in-one at the Bel Air Country Club in 1961 was "the greatest thrill in my life."

CHIP SHOT

The *Guinness Book of World Records* says that the most holes-in-one in a single round of golf was achieved by Patrick Wills in 2015 at the Laurel Hill Golf Club in Lorton, Virginia. He shot three aces!

Not-So Memorable Moments

At the 1990 Australian Open, Brett Ogle had his kneecap broken by his ball after it deflected off a tree.

❖

Gary Player was on his way to defending his Masters championship in 1962 when an overzealous fan with an iron grip shook his hand and sprained it. Player was forced to play the final round with a bandaged hand and eventually lost a play-off to Arnold Palmer.

❖

Lee Trevino was leading the final round of the 1970 British Open by three strokes, but pulled a colossal boner on the fifth hole when he hit the ball to the wrong stick. He never recovered and Jack Nicklaus wound up the winner.

❖

Bob Rosburg missed a three-foot putt on the 72nd hole to lose the U.S. Open by one stroke to Orville Moody.

❖

Sam Snead once drove a ball into the pocket of a man who was standing nearly 250 yards away.

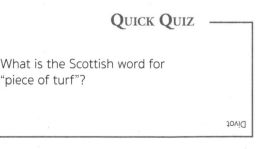

QUICK QUIZ

What is the Scottish word for "piece of turf"?

Divot

In 1985, *Golf Digest* sponsored a tournament which would determine the worst avid golfer in the U.S. The winner (or loser, more appropriately) was Angelo Spangola of Fayette City, Pennsylvania. On the 17th hole, a 138-yard par-3, Spagnola shot 66, hitting 27 balls into the water. He finished with a 257, 49 strokes more than the "runner-up."

❖

Back in the day, the folks at the Hillcrest Country Club in Beverly Hills once considered revoking the memberships of comedians George Burns and Harpo Marx for playing a round of golf in their whitey tighties.

❖

At the 1988 Canadian Open, Dave Bally had an easy putt but as he approached his ball, he tripped, sending his putter flying into the ball and knocking it off the green into a nearby pond. He wound up with a triple bogey on the par-3 hole.

❖

Golf pro Homero Blancas was in the rough, carefully lined up his shot and then hit the ball. It bounced off a palm tree and landed in the bra of a spectator. Blancas conferred with Chi Chi Rodriguez as to what he should do and Rodriguez replied, "I think you should play it."

CHIP SHOT

At the Kampala Golf Club in Uganda, you're allowed free relief from hippopotamus footprints. Golfers are also warned to avoid water hazards on ten of the eighteen holes where there's a danger of crocodiles.

Judy Rankin looked like she had the 1979, $150,000 LPGA Tournament locked up. She held a five-shot lead after the 3rd round but then things started to slip. It all came down to a critical putt on the 17th. Just as she drew her putter back, a fly landed on the ball. Some deep reflex in Rankin's brain must have signaled swat because she whacked the ball so hard it went flying way past the hole, costing her the lead and the tournament.

❖

In 1996, Scott Browning of Houston, Texas, suffered a ruptured achilles tendon at a men's club sponsored golf tournament and was awarded $16,500 in damages. Browning was injured when an exotic dancer who was assigned to be his "designated caddie" and cart driver got so tipsy she overturned their cart into a drainage canal.

❖

Scotland's Raymond Russell was certain that he was going to finish in a top spot. However, going into the last round of the 2001 Compass English Open at the Marriott Forest of Arden, his hopes were, shall we say, sunk. At the 17th green, he threw his ball to the caddy for cleaning. The caddy missed the toss and was horrified as the ball rolled into the lake. The ball couldn't be found, resulting in a two-stroke penalty and 4,500 pounds in lost prize money!

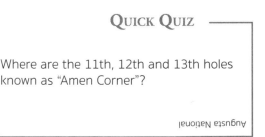

QUICK QUIZ

Where are the 11th, 12th and 13th holes known as "Amen Corner"?

Augusta National

Military Mayhem

Lee Trevino once said that he played "World War II golf - out in 39 and back in 45." While that may get a chuckle, the folks at the St. Mellons Golf and Country Club in England were very serious about the war and posted the following rules:

• Players are asked to collect bomb and shrapnel splinters found on the course.

• In competition, during gunfire, or while bombs are falling, players may take shelter without penalty for ceasing play.

• A ball moved by enemy action may be replaced, or if lost or destroyed, a ball may be dropped without penalty, not nearer the hole.

• A player whose stroke is affected by the explosion of a bomb may play another ball under penalty of one stroke.

Duffer's Dearest

The first woman to write a book about golf was Mrs. Edward Kennard. In 1896, she penned the text which was titled *The Sorrows of a Golfer's Wife*.

CHIP SHOT

For those in the "kneed to know," Shinobu Saeki set the world record for- you guessed it -driving a golf ball while kneeling. His shot traveled 255 yards, 2 inches at a Japanese course in 2019.

Hitting Spectators is Easy...
Shooting Down a Plane is Hard

In Livermore, California, a golfer who got a bit too much loft managed to send his ball through the windshield of a small plane in the process of landing at a nearby airport. Although the pilot took a terrific crack to the noggin, the plane touched down safely, which goes to prove that flying is safer than driving.

An Ace for the Ages

Andrew Magee holds the record for the longest hole-in-one in a PGA tournament. He set the mark in 2001 at the Phoenix Open in Scottsdale, Arizona, on the par-4 17th hole- 332 yards.

Nice Shot

Golfer Bob Russell took a practice shot on a municipal course in Ohio in 1974 and felt a terrible pain in his leg. The head of his driver hit a bullet that someone had carelessly left behind. Fortunately, the wound was minor- although it did ruin a perfectly good pair of golf pants.

QUICK QUIZ

What are the five majors in women's professional golf?

ANA Inspiration, Women's PGA Championship, U.S. Women's Open, Women's British Open and Evian Championship

Thoughts of the Throne

• Lee Trevino, talking of the similar roots he and Seve Ballesteros share, once said, "We come from the same backgrounds, more or less, where growing up next to a golf course didn't mean a 10,000-square foot house and gold faucets in the bathroom."

• While SuperMex was on the PGA tour in 1968, he visited The Alamo, in San Antonio, Texas. Trevino was heard to say, "Well, I'm not gonna buy this place. It doesn't have indoor plumbing."

• An exhausted Fuzzy Zoeller, after 36 holes on the final rain-delayed day of the 1981 Colonial National Invitation tournament said, "It was a very long day. I don't know how long we've been out there, but I know it's time to shave again."

• When golfer Johnny Pott was introduced at the Los Angeles Open in the 1960s, the announcer committed this blooper: "Now on the pot, Johnny Tee."

• Joyce Kasmierski, on network television at the 1983 Women's Kemper Open, said this about weather conditions: "The wind was so strong there were whitecaps in the porta-john."

CHIP SHOT

When the Talamore Golf Course opened in 1991 in Pinehurst, North Carolina, golfers were offered the opportunity to purchase a llama as their caddy. The animals were capable of carrying two golf bags each and cost $200 per round.

Ode to the 19th Hole

"N is for nineteenth, the hole that's the best,
And the reason some golfers play all of the rest."

-From *Golf is a Four-Letter Word*,
by Richard Armour

The Bathroom Library

For more information:

Email - info@Red-LetterPress.com
Website - www.Red-LetterPress.com